THE PROMOTIONAL EDGE

The Complete Guide to the Successful Oral Interview

Ronald S. Bateman

Harry C. Mounts, Jr.

THIRD EDITION

PROMOTIONAL EDGE PUBLISHING
ANNAPOLIS • MARYLAND

THE
PROMOTIONAL EDGE
The Complete Guide to the Successful Oral Interview

All Rights Reserved
Ronald S. Bateman and Harry C. Mounts, Jr.
Copyright © 1998
3rd Edition

PROMOTIONAL EDGE PUBLISHING
ANNAPOLIS • MARYLAND

Copyright © 1994, 1st Edition
Copyright © 1996, 2nd Edition

Printed in the USA by:
Morris Publishing
3212 East Highway, Kearney, NE 68847

ISBN 0-9663652-0-8

Library of Congress Catalog Card Number: 98-91379

> Promotional Edge Publishing books are available at quantity discounts for educational, business, or sales promotional use. For information, please write to: Promotional Edge Publishing, Special Sales Depatment, 626-C Suite 220, Admiral Drive, Annapolis, Maryland 21401

All rights reserved. No part of this book may be reproduced in any form or by any electronic or mechanical means including photocopying, recording, or by any information storage and retrieval system without expressed written permission from the authors and publisher, except for inclusion of brief quotations in a review or article. This publication is provided as a research service to its readers and while a conscientious and professional effort is made to ensure accuracy of the contents, no warranty is expressed or implied.

*Dedicated
to
helping you achieve success.*

THE PROMOTIONAL EDGE

AUTHOR'S NOTE

Most would agree that few colleges or companies actually prepare students for the various phases of the hiring process. Whether it be for promotion or to be hired most people test several times before they realize their weaknesses, and learn how to be a top contender. So what does this amount to? Some say it's a learning process, we say it's a waste of time. Therefore, it's imperative to educate yourself another way. That's where Chuck and I come in.

In 1994, after seeing my informal instruction pay off for several people, I designed the first edition booklets for both the oral and written exams. Seeing good potential employees and leaders being hired and promoted from their hard work and my self-taught information was exciting. My driving goal was, and still is, to teach future leaders what has taken me years to learn, thus giving them an *edge* over their competition. That's how I came up with name, *The Promotional Edge.*

Chuck and I share the same hard core studying philosophies, which made it easy to write the second and third editions. We both know that this strenuous process allows only a few to succeed and many left to try again. Those that are hired or promoted are part of a small percentage that are totally devoted. Like we were, those people are easy to pick out. They are serious, focused, confident and determined. Chuck and I both agree that no book, no person, and no college course will do it all for you. Instead, you hold the key to your own success, it's called hard work. Remember, you can never compromise success. To reach your dreams you must be totally committed and put forth your best to achieve your dreams.

Ronald S. Bateman

AUTHOR'S NOTE

You have taken the first step in achieving your dream. Securing your chosen career or promotion is within your power and ability. You have already set your goal. Now you must formulate a strategy and execute that strategy with determination. This book is designed to help you with your strategy and guide you through the process with the fundamental components of achieving your goal.

Beginning as an idea of Ron's several years ago, we got together to formulate a packet of information to help others in getting promoted by concentrating on the oral interview process. The result was a fifty-page booklet (the first edition) written by Ron. During our research in compiling our information we found that we shared the same philosophy, ideas, and techniques used in getting promoted. Now several years and two editions later, we have combined our efforts and expanded the material once again, the result is this book - the third edition.

We haven't forgotten the tremendous amount of time, energy, and effort it takes in preparing for an oral interview. We understand the hard work involved in reaching your goal as we have gone through the process ourselves. I, for one, have failed the oral interview during the promotional process, but I learned from my mistakes and have come out number-one in later years. I strongly believe you can achieve anything you want if you are willing to pay the price. Don't trust your goals to luck. Rather, trust your future achievements to hard work, tenacity, and a positive mental attitude. Have confidence in your abilities and you will succeed.

Chuck Mounts

Table of Contents

INTRODUCTION	1
STRESS	2
PREPARATION	3
POWER WORDS	4
THE CRITIQUE	5
BODY LANGUAGE	6
THE ASSESSMENT	7
TYPES OF INTERVIEWS	8
DRESSING SHARP	9
THE BIG DAY	10
INTERVIEW QUESTIONS	11
INTERVIEWING TIPS	12
MOCK ORAL INTERVIEW	13
CONCLUSION	14
FINAL NOTE	15
INDEX	16

Introduction

The oral interview is one of the most important steps in the sometimes difficult process of getting hired or promoted. This book reveals the building blocks to a successful oral interview, ranging from the strategies and techniques of interviewing to sample dialogue and research tips. Some may ask why mastering the art of interviewing is so important. We say this --- no matter how well you do in other aspects of career seeking or job enhancement, your efforts will be futile if you fail to do your best in today's competitive market, and you will not be competitive until you leap the hurdles of the job interview. Once you're inside an office and engaged in an interview, your entire future may rest upon how well you present yourself to a stranger sitting behind a desk across from you in an average time span of approximately thirty minutes.

Unlike many other career searching manuals, this book is dedicated solely to the oral interviewing process. The following scenario stresses the importance of the oral interview.

The young job seeker opened the glass office door and walked briskly across the doorway. The man's body language reflected his inner most feelings. He held his head high and grinned like a Cheshire cat as he nodded at the receptionist sitting behind the desk before shuffling into the office. The man was proud of the fact he had just completed his graduate studies. He was the Big-Man-On-Campus. Mr. A-Number-One. Mr. Numero Uno.

1-2   THE PROMOTIONAL EDGE

The man stood erect at the walnut-veneer table positioned in front of the interviewer before taking a seat inside the small conference room. He looked at his watch and smiled as he thought about his new position. He found a cynical inner peace with the fact that the other interviewees waiting down the hall for their names to be called seemed uneasy and nervous.

The man's face wrinkled into a devious smirk as he thought of all the hard work, time, and effort the other interviewees must have gone through preparing for this day. He didn't have to prepare for any interview. He knew all the answers. His hard work paid off during his college days. He was captain of the chess team and a straight-A student with an MBA degree. They would be begging for him to take a job with their company. What more could somebody possibly ask him? Besides, the interviewer was only going to ask him a couple of questions and he'd be out of there in about twenty minutes.

"How hard could this be? I'm Mr. Numero Uno," he reassured himself.

The personnel director, an attractive woman dressed in a blue business suit, politely asked the man to tell her a little something about himself. The man rested his elbow on the armrest and slouched back into the padded chair. He thought to himself for a moment, "Boy, this is going to be like taking candy from a baby. Better make myself comfortable." The man crossed his legs and exposed his bare ankle as his pants rode up his thick hairy leg.

The man cleared his throat before he began his dissertation and coughed as the woman leaned back in her chair in an attempt to distance herself from the attack of mucus germs that had now radiated throughout the room.

The man toyed with the wide lapel on his red, plaid sportscoat as he answered the question, "Well Missy, let me tell you something. I've done well for myself in school, and know everything there is to know about this job. I was pretty popular in college, and everybody knows I know how to do the job. Sometimes you have to shoot from the hip to get what ya want, if you get my meaning. But hey, it's all just part of the game." The man was pleased with his response as he watched the woman with an opened mouth, stare back at him. He was confident that the woman was impressed by his hard line delivery, yet gentle approach, by referring to her as, "Missy."

"Yeap, I could always size up them kinda women," he said to himself.

Suddenly a barrage of questions was fired at the man in quick succession. He grabbed at the collar of his wrinkled, stained shirt as he tried to stutter a response. The man needed more time to formulate his answers. He panicked as the questions began to pile up. The man's thoughts reeled around in his mind like an unbalanced washing machine. Suddenly, the room felt hot and stuffy. The florescent overhead lights caused him to perspire profusely. Beads of sweat rolled down the sides of his plump red face. His pupils became dilated as his body shifted in his seat. His feet were now planted firmly on the floor as he sat erect against the back of the chair. The man scratched his head as he wrinkled his forehead in thought, but his mind went blank. The smirk on his face had long disappeared. He was always so self-assured, but somehow this was different.

Adrenaline pumped through his veins. The old fight-or-flight syndrome began to kick in as he quickly scanned the room for a rescue party. He thought of escape, but was trapped by his predatory inquisitor. Suddenly, through the blinding glare of the overhead lights he heard a hope of relief from his torturous examiner, "Our time is almost up. Is there anything else you would like to say?"

Bizarre thoughts of public disgrace and humiliation flashed through his mind. Quickly, the man attempted to adapt to the questioning technique. Alas, it was too late. The interviewer *stood at the table and extended her hand, "Thank you, for your time. We'll call you if anything becomes available."*

The man slowly shuffled out of the room with his head bowed in defeat as he murmured his thoughts of despair, "Maybe I should have prepared a little more."

Is this scenario an exaggerated rendition of an oral interview? Well maybe, but we hope we've made our point. The need for proper preparation and practice, not to mention confidence, articulation, enthusiasm, and the proper control of body language just to name a few, are indicative of a proper oral presentation. The oral interview is your opportunity to demonstrate your self-assurance and confidence by conveying your thoughts, work habits, and management abilities in a positive and professional manner. Your spoken words are just as important as your nonverbal communication skills. This is very important to remember. Experts have estimated that as much as 93% of the emotional content of speech is conveyed by nonverbal clues. Therefore, those subtle things like facial expressions, varying your vocal variety and pitch, along with the effective use of gestures all play a part in communicating your message. Coupled together, they provide clues to the interviewer of your intentions, interest, work and management potential. You must communicate to the interviewer by your words and nonverbal demeanor that you will not be a liability, but a valuable asset to the company.

REVITALIZING YOUR CONFIDENCE

By now you have probably searched the classified ads, formulated your resume, networked with friends, and completed countless job applications in your search for that perfect career. With all of that completed, you will eventually be asked to interview for the position for which you are seeking. Once you're scheduled for an interview, you will probably only know the location, time, and maybe the length of the interview, and nothing else. You have no idea what questions an interviewer may ask you, and there isn't anything you can do to prepare. Right? *Wrong!* We believe there is very much to do before the interview, yet very few job seekers properly prepare or have ever been trained in the art of oral interviewing.

The first thing you must do prior to the oral interview is to revitalize your confidence. Regardless of how you have performed on past interviews, college tests, or prior jobs, you must now face a whole new phase. In fact, it is a phase where many fail due to the lack of confidence. A lack of confidence, quite simply, stems from the lack of preparation, practice, and belief in yourself. Your level of confidence has a direct effect on how well you present your responses to interview questions and how well they are received by the interviewer. The amount of preparation and practice you put forth prior to the interview is directly proportionate to the display of confidence and the correctness of your answers during the interview. You must know what employers expect from good employees. This will help you convince employers that you are the right person for the job. Knowing what to expect is one of the best ways to increase your confidence and decrease your anxiety level.

PREPARING FOR THE UNKNOWN

So, how do you prepare for the unknown? Interviewing requires solid preparation. First and foremost, you must understand that the oral interview process is not as much of an unknown as it may appear. Unless the company or whomever you are going to interview with is going to try something totally irrelevant, most oral interviews are similar in structure and basic content. This is done for a reason. The main purpose of an oral interview is to measure a potential employee's personality traits, work habits, and supervisory potential. To do this, a series of questions are asked, deliberately designed to cause the interviewee to show their work potential, and to bring about their abilities to think and act like qualified employees or managers. Research has shown that the four main reasons why most fail the interviewing process is for one or more of the following reasons listed on the following page:

> **REASONS FOR FAILING AN INTERVIEW**
>
> - 40% Poor appearance
> - 80% Can't identify job related skills
> - 80% Can't effectively communicate
> - 90% Can't answer questions to an employer's satisfaction

With this said, your preparation is vital and you must focus on the areas most commonly assessed (explained in later chapters). Many virtuous interviewees will go through the interview process, but only those who properly prepare will get hired or promoted.

BENEFITS TO PREPARATION

Is preparation necessary? Will it help? Isn't it all luck? Luck is when preparation and opportunity meet. The degree in which you prepare for the oral interview will determine your confidence level and arm you with a comprehensive file of information from which you can draw upon to give complete and thorough responses. The other added benefit from preparation is to help you in the manner in which you deliver your responses, with the goal of being articulate, logical, well poised, and able to supplement your responses with examples. After all, if you can remember the basic content of your high school speech class, short illustrated examples turn good responses into great ones. Short illustrations allow the listener to get a clear picture of what is being said, which in turn reveals your specific and overall knowledge on the subject matter.

Many successful people attribute their success to preparation. In an analogy regarding preparation, many respected and successful attorneys in a court of law liken themselves to magicians with hundreds of tricks up their sleeves, not knowing which one they will need, but ready to pull out any one at any given time. They are successful because they are ready for any eventuality. They take the time to analyze every situation and possible question or option. They are prepared.

The most useful and reassuring fact we can give you right now, is that the examiners who are conducting the interview want you to succeed. Their job is to establish an eligibility list of qualified applicants, and they will be most satisfied with their work if they believe that each interviewee can succeed in the position for which they were interviewed. It is important to note, however, that although the interviewers are primarily looking for strengths and assets of the interviewee, the interviewers must also take into account any deficiencies they discover. Your job is to correct those deficiencies prior to your scheduled interview and to keep them from falling face-first on the interview table. Whatever your general and specific qualifications may be, the hurdle of the oral interview is still ahead. Your success or failure in the interview will depend largely upon how well you have prepared, practiced, and how well you handle yourself.

As you approach the time of the oral interview, you will be naturally concerned with many questions. How well will you be received? What if you fail? What does my competition have over me? What questions will be asked? How can you possibly prepare for an interview when you don't have any idea of the line of attack you will face? Maybe it would be wise for you to withdraw your application and wait for a better time, and a better opportunity when you will be better prepared. You may feel, as others do, that this is a highly unequal contest. All the weapons, strategies, and initiatives are stacked in favor of the interviewers, right? *Wrong!*

First, what is the reason for an oral interview? Is it to test your technical knowledge? Generally speaking, the answer is no. Technical knowledge is the job skills one possesses. Your technical knowledge will be or has already been tested in a written examination depending on the company or the type of job you are seeking. However, some interviews do test some parts of your technical knowledge coupled with your conceptual skills. The higher you move up the corporate ladder, the less likely you will use your technical knowledge. The hands-on skills of accomplishing tasks are left for subordinates, the worker-bees. As you move up the chain of command, you will accomplish your goals through your conceptual knowledge by getting things done through the people you supervise. We are referring to the conceptual knowledge of planning, organizing, staffing, setting goals, coordinating your efforts, and motivating employees.

KNOWLEDGE BASE

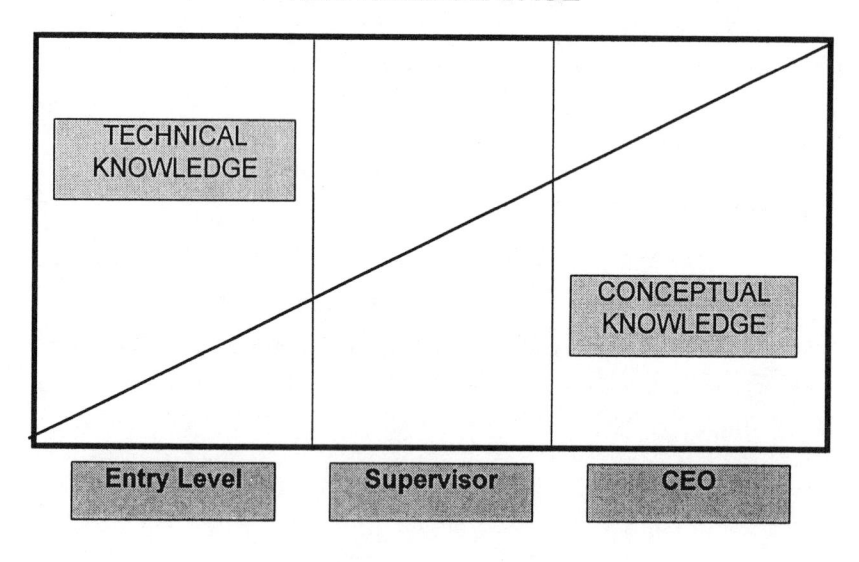

[Diagram: A rectangular chart with a diagonal line rising from lower-left to upper-right. "TECHNICAL KNOWLEDGE" box is in the upper-left; "CONCEPTUAL KNOWLEDGE" box is in the lower-right. Below the chart are three labels: "Entry Level", "Supervisor", "CEO".]

Prior to an interview and even with a detailed written resume, many questions affecting job success have not yet been evaluated. Again, your conceptual knowledge. Some of these areas include: quality of work experience and training, stability, ambition, ability to work with others, communication skills, manner, speech, interpersonal skills, decision making, and the general impression created by your appearance. The interviewer must rate these traits on the basis of what they can learn from you during a relatively brief period of time. For this reason, every little clue and impression you give an interviewer during the interview is crucial.

The techniques of interviewing haven't changed much since Moe hired Larry and Curly, and the oral interview isn't the Dark Hole everyone makes it out to be, but you must prepare yourself, or you will find yourself trying to climb out of that Dark Hole, interview after interview. Granted, there are an infinite number of scenarios or questions that an interviewer can throw at you to answer, but you can use the finite number of basic Problem Solving Techniques (explained in the following chapters) to formulate your responses. Understanding and knowing what attributes the interviewers will score you on will also greatly improve your interview score. This is part of what we will teach you and what you will learn from this book. The interview process becomes much easier when you understand the rules of the game. Trying to beat the odds at a Las Vegas Casino card game becomes much easier when you understand the rules of the game (research) and practice playing poker (preparation) before sitting down at a card table, than if you have never seen a deck of cards before.

Studying the interview principles and strategies in this book, and applying the techniques will not necessarily get you hired or promoted without hard work. It will, however, at the very least, improve your confidence and vastly improve your overall oral interview presentation.

Some of the information you will receive in this book will be repeated throughout the chapters, but we want to stress the information we believe is important for a successful interview. Study the different checklists presented throughout the book for quick reference guides, as well as the do's and don'ts of interviewing. Be sure to review the last couple of chapters in the back of the book including the oral interview questions and the mock interview scoring sheets as these chapters will be quite beneficial to you. Make copies of them and use them during your mock oral interviews. Now, roll up your sleeves and get ready to go to work.

Luck –
"Luck is when preparation and opportunity meet."

Stress 2

Don't overlook this chapter. It is included because we understand and still recall the amount of time and effort it takes in order for you to reach your goal. Rest assured preparing for the oral interview will be very trying at times. Most likely there will be times when you will wonder if it is all worth it. It is, but you must hang in there. It is all part of bearing the price of success. The competitive nature of seeking out a career or getting promoted brings on a whole new meaning to stress. As you will see, if you haven't already, you will not only endure internal stress, but stress from your peers, friends, and family. For the next couple of weeks prepare yourself and your family to wage a cerebral battle during your oral interviewing study phase. To achieve victory, you must understand your strengths and vulnerabilities. To do this you must develop a successful counter strategy and instill in yourself a winning attitude.

Our mental processes are more predictable than we care to admit and the more you understand the impending threat to your emotional well being, the better your defenses will be. Some anxieties are bound to affect you even if you don't expect it or deny they exist.

Today, nearly everything we do creates stress in one form or another. Being stuck in traffic or running late for a doctor's appointment are examples of stressful situations. The very daily existence in life has changed so much that time, overcrowding, and everyday worries make stress an inescapable fact of life.

You will experience increased stress while job hunting. This is a normal occurrence that we all have experienced at one time or another, but the frequency and duration of the stress will of course, vary with your personality, future outlook, self-esteem, family support, history, environment, and physical health.

THE EARLY WARNING SIGNS

Stress can set off feelings of despair and depression. Harmful stress may not only damage your psychological well being, but may manifest itself in a variety of physical signs and symptoms as well. Some of the most common indicators of stress, if not released, are headaches, neck and back pains, heartburn, stomach pains, and increased susceptibility to infections. Prolonged exposure to stressful situations can have an adverse effect on your health, but stress can also be beneficial. Stress triggers the body's safety mechanisms, allowing you to handle many of life's unplanned occurrences. In planned occurrences, such as skydiving or off-road racing, stress can prompt feelings of exhilaration and ecstasy that one feels. Stress can also improve your daily productivity, energizing you to meet tight deadlines and deal effectively with tough problems. We both agree that as the interview day approached when we were preparing for our promotional interviews during our career, we seemed to study better and comprehend more information. However, others have stated to us it has an opposite effect on them. The closer to the deadline of the oral interview the harder it seemed for them to concentrate. Whatever the case, we all feel the pressure when attempting to achieve our goals.

The sense and feelings of stress are as old as man himself, and are built into our genetic make-up. The old fashioned word for it was called tension. Scientists now believe that the amount of stress a person experiences may not necessarily lead to further anxieties. The leading culprit is a person's inability to recognize and control stressful situations. Your success in staying physically and mentally healthy depends greatly on your ability to identify those stresses that are preventable, avoidable, and controllable.

You must focus your energies on effectively managing those stresses that you cannot prevent, but can control. Case in point, the oral interview.

Stress affects people differently, and even the same pressure will affect a person differently at different times. Some anxieties may not occur while other anxieties may occur in different order or intensity. Stress can be expressed emotionally as fear, resentment, anxiety, anger, or abrupt mood changes. Your family and friends can help alert you to any major behavioral changes. Listen to their assessment of your behavior and then act on it in a positive manner.

One internal source of stress is *anticipatory stress*, where an unpleasant or uncomfortable upcoming event can cause fear or anxiety beforehand, such as your scheduled oral interview. These events seem to reach out from the future and bother us before they even occur. Other sources of stress are *time stress* where we feel the pressure to accomplish something before a deadline and *situational stress* where we perceive a situation to be threatening.

The important thing to remember is that most of your reactions will be normal. However, what is normal for you depends on how you interpret the experience. You must develop a mental attitude of *"I CAN"* rather than an *"I CAN'T"* state of mind. The *I CAN* state of mind is empowering and successful, whereas the *I CAN'T* mindset will never accomplish very much of anything.

Take charge and control each situation you encounter. Don't worry about the little problems, they always work themselves out. To control stress, you must control the irritants that affect us in everyday life. For example, take the irritant of an oyster. A grain of sand that works its way underneath the tough exterior of an oyster's shell becomes an irritant to the oyster's soft insides. The oyster responds to the uncomfortable feeling by creating a smooth, protective coating that surrounds the grain of sand. The outcome turns an irritant into something great --- a pearl. Like the oyster, *how* we face our problems will determine future outcome. The sources of stress we create for ourselves reside neither in the situation nor the person, but result in the interaction of the two. Stress is not caused by outside forces, but by our own ideas about them, our perception, and what they mean to us. Quite simply, YOU control the stress you feel.

POINTS TO REMEMBER

- ☺ **Confide in Your Family and Friends** - Don't shut out your support group. Tell them what you are undertaking and feeling. They will understand and can help you achieve your goal as well as do wonders for your confidence. One of the most powerful protections against the pressures of stress is the closeness of a spouse or friend.

- ☺ **Believe in Yourself** - and you will succeed. Make it a daily goal to tell yourself - *I WILL GET HIRED* or *I WILL GET PROMOTED*. Write it down on an index card, and carry it with you always. Read it, say it aloud, and visualize it. Believe it and it will happen. You can control your own destiny.

- ☺ **Be Good to Yourself** - A grueling study time can cause burnout. Study hard, but put time aside for you and your family. Use the time as a reward for your hard work. Prevent self-inflicted stress by dedicating some time to just relaxing. It will help recharge your batteries, and your renewed energy will allow you to become more focused. Put pleasure into your everyday life and give yourself something to look forward to.

- ☺ **Think Positive** - Be optimistic. Don't be afraid of failure. The fear of failure is one of the biggest causes of mental strain. Indecision creates tension, thus cultivate decisiveness. Remember, you control your own mental well being and emotional stress level. Positive vibrations are contagious. Take charge and gain autonomy over your life by controlling your own destiny.

- ☺ **Exercise** - Extra physical activity will reduce your tension and anxiety. Jog or take a stroll around your neighborhood. The quiet time can be used to clear your thoughts.

- ☺ **Stay Healthy** - Eat a well-balanced diet of nutritional foods. Keep your body properly fueled to handle the increased mental anxiety. Physical stamina and the degree to which we keep our bodies healthy is an important factor in stress management.

- ☺ **Sleep Well** - Maintain a regular sleeping schedule. Sleep is nature's way of healing your mind and body. Give yourself the opportunity to rest. Sleep improves alertness and the retention of information. It also helps maintain a good sense of humor. Don't ever lose your sense of humor. You must be able to laugh at yourself and the crazy torture that you will be putting yourself through.

- ☺ **Relax Mentally** - It is important to remember the human body is not a machine when developing a proper attitude toward the pressures of attaining your goal. Get into a relaxed frame of mind before you begin studying.

Studying, preparation, and practice requires a quiet, calm environment, free from distractions. This environment will help you concentrate on your preparation, and keep your mind clear. The art of mental relaxation is to rest the mind. Your preparation for the oral interview will be trying. Get away from it all if it becomes too overbearing, or take a quick break by trying an effective relaxation exercise. Stop what you are doing and find a quiet place for about ten minutes. Sit quietly in a comfortable position. Close your eyes and visualize being in a peaceful setting. Think about a gentle spring rainfall or a tranquil green meadow, or imagine yourself gazing up at the brilliant stars on a cool summer night. This is your relaxation fantasy, so you control the scenery. Gently, but deeply, inhale through your nose and slowly exhale through your mouth. Pause for a few seconds between each breath. Become aware of your own natural rhythms. Let your body take control. Deeply relax all of your muscles beginning at your feet and progress up to your face.

As you sit in your imaginary world of complete harmony, use your mind's eye to visualize each part of your body starting to relax. Begin with your toes and work your way up to your head. As you let out each breath, feel each part of your body start to relax. Mentally visualize and physically feel each muscle relaxing as your inner tension starts to dissolve away. Continue these thoughts and feelings until your entire body is relaxed. When you have completed the exercise, your whole body will become relaxed and your mind clear. You will emerge with renewed spirits and a feeling of self-control. You may even discover yourself waking up from a short nap, with a puddle of drool nearby. It's okay, and maybe a time to laugh at yourself. It may take a few attempts to become accustomed to this routine, but it does work. When beginning this technique, don't worry about whether you have achieved a deep level of relaxation. Permit the relaxation to occur at its own pace. With practice, the method will come with little effort.

Okay, now, get back to work. The following chapters are the nuts and bolts of the oral interviewing process.

Self-confidence -
"Self-confidence is the requisite to great undertakings."
Samuel Johnson (1709-1784) English Poet

Preparation 3

SCHEDULING

You should carefully plan your study schedule days in advance, and in writing, all the way until the Big Day. To do this, determine when you will work on your Opening and Closing Statements, when you will visit the oral interview location, when you will work on formulating scenarios, questions and answers, when you will be reading various management and oral communication books (such as this one), conducting your mock interview on video, and when you will be reviewing or discussing questions and answers with a friend or partner. Place a personal calendar in plain view as a reminder of what you intend to accomplish each day. Write it down and stick to it. Treat it like homework, paying a bill, or whatever you like, but get it done.

Scheduling your preparation will help reduce your level of stress by showing you in black and white that your plan is mapped out. It will also keep your mind from thinking about what else you must do. Secondly, it forces you to cover each step and not ignore another. So don't be one of those people who talk a big show about preparation, but only completes half of what is desired. Remember, your preparation will show during your oral interview.

VISITING THE ORAL INTERVIEW SITE

As soon as you are aware of the interview location, go to it and familiarize yourself with the surroundings. If you are permitted to enter the room, do so, and visualize yourself in the interview process, relaxed, full of enthusiasm and confidence, firing off great responses. Gauge how far your assessors will be sitting from you. Determine if the chair you may be sitting in has arms. See if there is a table leg that may be in your way. Spend some time in the room and get comfortable. This will be one less distraction that you will have to deal with on the Big Day.

Why should you bother to do all of this you may ask? It's simple. An unknown becomes a known, which in turn creates less stress and more familiarity. The more familiar you are with something, the more comfortable you become. Familiarity creates confidence.

UNDERSTANDING THE POSITION

Many job seekers who are applying for a position simply read an ad or job announcement, then submit an application or resume. They take for granted the job duties based on the position title and brief description provided. To walk into a job or promotion interview with only limited knowledge is asking for failure. One of your main objectives is to stand out from the rest, to be different in a positive light, and to make the interviewers want you on their team. To do this requires some research on your part. Take the extra time to investigate the position. Learn what the job entails, not just the written job description, but the responsibilities the position carries. This may require a little innovation, such as, talking with past and present employees, researching via the internet, obtaining a copy of the complete job description from the company, or whatever else your detective skills can uncover.

It is extremely important to understand how the position you are applying for relates to the rest of the organization. Knowing and communicating this during your interview will show you have a grasp on the big picture of the agency, not just the immediate position at hand. Employers want and need people who can envision the big picture. Being able to sell yourself with this trait will highlight your maturity, suggest creativity, and promote your growth and worth potential to the organization.

KNOW YOUR INTERVIEWERS

Just as the military gathers as much intelligence information as possible about its enemy before an attack, so must you. Football coaches and players watch game films of teams they are going up against next week, as do boxers readying themselves for an upcoming bout in order to gain some insight to their opponent's abilities. It is good to know something about the people who are assessing your qualities. Some companies will provide you with the names of the assessors and background information. If the company you are applying to does not provide a list of names of the persons sitting on the oral interview board, find out from others who will be interviewing you, if possible. Find out what latest innovative programs are hot in the company or field you are applying for and familiarize yourself with them. If you are provided with a resume of each panel member, pay close attention. What career path did the panel members take? Did they spend a good portion of their career in a field you have been in or are applying for? Has any portion of your career taken a similar path? Do you have future aspirations to seek similar assignments? What colleges or universities did they attend? What were their majors? Did you attend the same college? Is your major the same as one of the panel members? This intelligence information will arm you with information that will later assist you in the *bonding process* discussed later in this book. Gathering information and relating that information in preparing for your interview will go a long way. All of this may require additional research, but it will show you have done your homework during the interview.

RESEARCH POTENTIAL EMPLOYERS

It is important to research the potential companies or employers you are seeking to be hired by, as many company issues may come up during the interview process. The following are some suggestions you should consider while researching employer information for your benefit.

- Research the product line or service.
- Identify the company's competition and their strength.
- Where is the organization's corporate headquarters?
- Does the company offer a training program?
- What is the typical career path within the company?
- Who is the organization's chief executive officer?
- What are the philosophies of the organization?
- Find out the size of the firm or company, including the number of employees.
- What is the potential growth of the company and the industry it represents?
- Check the annual sales growth or expansion of services for the last several years.
- Does the company and position fit in with your employment objective?
- Stay informed of recent developments by reading daily newspapers, business magazines, and journals related to your career.

UPDATING YOUR ROLE AS A MANAGER

If it is a management position you are seeking, it is important that you refresh and update yourself as to your future role as a manager or supervisor. It is important to read different material to reacquaint yourself with key topics related to the position of a supervisor and manager. You must begin thinking like a manager in the truest sense of the word. To get yourself in the ideal manager mode of thinking, you will need to read selective management topics and really digest the material. Doing this will sharpen your intellectual skills and broaden your philosophy on management's role, thus enabling you to intelligently articulate your responses to an assessor's questions.

General topics and areas that will be beneficial to you are listed on the following page:

- Motivation
- Discipline
- Productivity
- Budgeting
- Personnel Complaints
- Personnel Grievances
- Handling Problem Employees
- Qualities of a Leader
- Leadership Principles
- Organizational Goals
- Problem Solving Techniques (important)

POLISHING UP ON YOUR COMMUNICATION SKILLS

There may be few of us who do a lot of public speaking and even fewer that have the natural ability to be an exceptional speaker, but we speak to people everyday. Do you remember your first day on the job speaking to the public? Were you a little nervous and unsure of yourself? Chances are you probably were. Now, you don't give it a second thought. You are in control and confident. Confidence comes from experience and practice. It is no different with public speaking. In fact, the majority of professional speakers become exceptional speakers, not by way of natural ability, but from research, preparation, experience, and practice. There are several easy-to-read public speaking books on the market today that can help sharpen your communication skills. Many of them offer helpful hints such as fluctuating your tone of voice to place emphasis on a particular word, the effective use of pausing, when to stop talking, the importance of short examples, the importance of incorporating simple, but vivid, power words for added conviction, and so on. This book will also assist you in these areas as outlined in later chapters.

OPENING AND CLOSING STATEMENTS

Many oral interviews will begin with an icebreaker question. You may be asked to give an overview about yourself and your career. This is a golden opportunity to deliver a well-polished, carefully prepared and practiced, Opening Statement. It is an excellent way to set the stage of the interview and make a strong impression. Without question, this is the easiest part of the interview. You are talking about the one you know best - YOU.

The technique recommended focuses on breaking your Opening Statement into easy to follow (for the interviewers), and easy to remember (for yourself) segments. The following is how you may want to design your custom-made Opening Statement.

The first step in preparing your Opening Statement is to make an outline consisting of three major areas. The first area should focus on your EDUCATIONAL background. The second area is to address your CAREER, and the last should cover miscellaneous POINTS OF INTEREST, such as awards received, specialized training, and other accomplishments. By structuring your outline and Opening Statement in this order, you will introduce yourself to the panel in an easy to follow format. This will aid the panel members in their note-taking task, and allow them to follow your Opening with relative ease. Regardless of how you organize your Opening Statement, avoid jumping from topic to topic as this will affect the assessors' comprehension and note-taking abilities. The assessors may have a lot of writing to do during this entire process, so make it easy for them to document the important points.

OPENING AND CLOSING HINTS

However you choose to organize your opening statement, place special emphasis on your knowledge, skills, abilities, and how you can be beneficial to the organization. If it is a promotion you are seeking, highlight the management and supervisory functions you have performed (i.e. developed policies, created training, served as acting supervisor, etc.).

Don't spend too much time talking about the awards you have received. What we mean is, don't dwell on what you have done in the past and have already been recognized for. If you over do it you may be perceived as showboating, so be careful. Experience is not what you have done, it is what you do with what you have done. You are not being rated on your current job, but on how you can help the organization in the present and future. What have you learned from these past experiences? What are your conceptual ideas? How will you use your new found knowledge? What are your management abilities?

Don't be afraid to toot your own horn. The important thing to remember is if you make a statement about yourself, back it up with statistics and examples. Stress the positive features about yourself, your accomplishments, and your strengths. If you say you are a good planner and organizer, talk briefly about some of the things that make you a good planner and organizer.

Some of the topics to bear in mind when creating your Opening Statement and Resume are:

- On-the-Job Training
- Awards
- Commendations
- Computer Proficiency
- Special Programs
- College Courses
- Scholastic Honors
- Professional Licenses
- Publications
- Presentations
- Training Certificates
- Foreign Languages
- Volunteer Work Related to your Employment
- Community Achievements
- Development of Projects
- Management of Resources
- Supervisory or Leadership of People
- Reduction in Expenditures
- Improvement in Quality of Services
- Improvement in Efficiency of Resources

The design and delivery of your Opening Statement is critical. To suggest that the introduction needs to be well planned is an understatement. Your Opening Statement must stimulate the interviewers and be full of information that will form the foundation of your credibility as a viable candidate for the position. Hence, the assessors have just made their third impression of you. What did we say, you ask? The Opening Statement is the *third* impression formed by the assessors? That's right. People will inherently start to form impressions of you (the first impression) as soon as you enter the doorway to the interview. The second impression is the introduction and handshake. The third, as we stated, is your Opening Statement. Let the interviewers know you have prepared yourself for the challenges of the position. If there is more than one interviewer, talk to each interviewer, not at them. Remain relaxed and let your confidence show through. Tell them what you are going to say, say it, then tell them what you have just said. As you begin designing your opening statement, start drafting an outline. Separate your outline into the major segments and then expound upon each.

For the following resume we have purposely taken a person with very basic and limited work experience to formulate our example. We did this to demonstrate how even a person with limited work exposure and education can be presented in the most favorable light. As you will see, it is all in *how* you say it. Those of you who possess more formidable credentials should be able to construct a much more impressive, action-oriented resume and opening statement. The following pages represent an example of a successful resume outline.

OUTLINING YOUR RESUME

I. Education
    A. Graduate of Chesapeake High School
    B. Associate of Arts Degree in Business from Anne Arundel Community College

    C.   Attending University of Maryland at Baltimore County (UMBC) - pursuing Bachelor of Arts Degree in Business Administration
    D.   Education provides a wider range of thinking, helps in problem solving

II.   Work Experience
    A.   Sales Clerk
        1. Responsible for accurate sales of merchandise and cash flow
        2. Responsible for friendly customer service
        3. Conducted daily merchandise receipts from vendors
        4. Priced merchandise and designed displays
        5. Excellent sick leave record
        6. Employee of the month (2 occasions)
    B.   Restaurant Assistant Manager
        1. Oversaw entire food service operation
        2. Handled/resolved customer complaints
        3. Responsible for motivating employees for maximum productivity
        4. Assisted with the discipline of problem employees (i.e. sick leave abuse, productivity complaints, etc.)
        5. Maintained food service/equipment supply
        6. Food service trainer
        7. Attended Management Training
        8. Recommended for upper management position

III.   Additional Points of Interest
    A.   Volunteer at Senior Center
    B.   Member of UMBC Business Club
- expands business knowledge, skills, trends
- broadening networking skills and resources

Once you have completed your outline, develop it into a crisp, powerful story about yourself. Use the Power Words you will find in the forthcoming chapters as you revise your resume into a final masterpiece. Design your Opening Statement into small paragraphs to help you learn the order of your material. When you have finished, go through your outline piece by piece, and put it into narrative form. Use small paragraphs that are full of vivid words, short examples, statistics, and so on. Generally, we don't speak the way we write, so be careful not to memorize each and every word. You may end up sounding like a broken record and lose the interviewers' attention. Remember, this is the third impression the panel members will have of you and it is crucial.

PRACTICING YOUR DELIVERY

Writing and reading something silently to yourself is one thing, but when it comes time to verbalize what you have just written out loud – *ouch!* Sometimes it just doesn't sound as well verbally. YOU MUST PRACTICE YOUR OPENING STATEMENT ALOUD. Not once, not twice, but over and over again. Get use to hearing yourself speak. Are your pauses full of *um's* and *ah's*, or do you have a smooth transition between sentences? Do you sound boring, or enthusiastic?

As you PRACTICE, PRACTICE, PRACTICE, think about where you may need to fluctuate your tone of voice for emphasis, and plug in useful gestures for added conviction. Speaking of gestures, let's touch on that briefly. There are some old-fashioned, not so-well-versed speakers that will tell you to never use your hands. We strongly disagree, as do most experts on oral communication. When used effectively, gestures add meaning and emphasis to your spoken words. Gestures should not distract your listener from what you are saying, but should serve as a nonverbal means to place importance on a topic or signal a transition in your speech.

Here is an example of what we mean. A close friend of ours was about to go through a video taped mock interview with us. Before the interview began we stood talking informally about his preparation and research. The way in which he communicated by using his hands, varying his tone, and incorporating great facial expressions, showed us he was going to be one of the best candidates we had ever interviewed. Soon thereafter we took our places and began the mock oral interview. After the first few minutes of the interview, we both almost fell out of our chairs. Here was a guy we have known for years, noted for his animation and enthusiasm, giving us this shallow, boring speech. Every time he went to lift his hands to make a gesture, he caught himself and quickly returned them to his lap. It was obvious he was preoccupied about not using his hands, rather than thinking about his responses. Soon, we too, became preoccupied with his body movements, rather than what he was saying. After the interview we questioned him about this. Just as we figured, someone had suggested that he not use his hands while speaking. Bad advice. He bombed our mock interview, but after pointing this out and working with him we are happy to say he is now a member of the upper-management staff.

Without this practice, our friend would have never known his shortcomings. Don't just practice alone, but practice in front of some of your close friends and family members. You will find that you will be more nervous in front of your friends than you will be in front of a stranger or two on the Big Day. Tell them to be critical of the manner in which you present your material as well as the content. Is this embarrassing for some? Yes, but we both cannot emphasize how important it is to get feedback. You will not only be practicing your Opening Statement aloud, but also your responses to mock questions that we will discuss later.

As the forthcoming example illustrates, begin each of the major sections with your category heading, *education*, *career*, *points of interest*, and then number each paragraph. When you begin practicing, you should work on one category at a time, focusing only on a couple of numbered paragraphs each time.

Work on delivering each category separately, then work on the next category, *without* including the first, and then the third, fourth, and so on. Once you feel comfortable with the content of each category, start bringing them together. First, present category #1 with category #2. Be sure to incorporate good verbal and nonverbal transitions as you change gears and move to a new category. Eventually, bring them all together, ending with a power-packed closing sentence or two in your Opening Statement.

OPENING STATEMENT (sample response)

To bring some logic to my resume I'd like to break this into three segments. First, I'll go over my education, then I'll give you an overview of my work experience, and lastly I'll touch on a few points of interest.

Education

- To begin with my education, I graduated from Chesapeake High School in the top 10% of my class.
- I continued my education out of high school and graduated from the Anne Arundel Community College with an Associate Arts Degree in Business Administration.
- I am presently attending University of Maryland, pursuing my Bachelor of Science Degree in Business Administration.
- I plan to continue my education as it will keep me fresh on current business and management issues, and expose me to the latest cutting edge business techniques and marketing trends.

Career

- Now for my work experience. My first employment was as a sales clerk for a large department store. This was my first true exposure to the business world, and the time I became aware of the importance of customer service. As a sales clerk, I

was responsible for the daily accurate sales of merchandise, receiving orders from vendors for the corporation, pricing and stocking merchandise and designing attractive customer displays to increase sales.
- In the two years at the company I received recognition for using only one sick day.
- I also received the Employee of the Month Award on two occasions.
- Working as a sales person provided me with a number of responsibilities surrounding accurate accounting and cash flow, and utilizing effective time management skills in order to accomplish several tasks.
- My sales experience challenged me to broaden my skills further and I took on my current employment as an Assistant Manager in the food service industry. As an Assistant Manager I first attended a three week management-training course, which was followed by three weeks of on the job training.
- My responsibilities included assisting the manager in overseeing the entire food service operation which is a very demanding task. I enjoy my position and have found it rewarding to train new employees to be responsible and courteous to the customers, and do their best, regardless of the job they are performing. As an Assistant Manager, I'm required for the scheduling of the staff, which includes both young employees, and seniors.
- I am required to motivate my staff to maximize their work output and assist the manager with disciplinary matters, along with handling customer complaints. I believe I have established excellent motivational techniques by the way in which I communicate to the staff, and always try to lead by example, showing them the importance of doing your best and how working as a team can reduce the individual work load and be fun.

Additional Points of Interest

- Outside of my work experiences and education, there are additional points that will be of interest to you. For the past five years, I have enjoyed assisting as a volunteer at the Annapolis Senior Center. I like helping seniors with organizing and participating in their learning and what we call their "Fun Day" activities. I've always had a special place in my heart for our seniors.
- Additionally, I am a member of the Business Club at the University of Maryland. The club keeps me up to date on the current business trends. My training and research as a result of this club has broadened my knowledge and skills. It has also allowed me to increase my networking capabilities and resources in the business community.

Conclusion

- If I could bring what I have said all together in just a few words let me emphasize this. I look forward to becoming a part of the team here at the Anne Arundel Medical Center. I feel strongly that my background, education, management, and customer service experiences have prepared me to provide the level of service and commitment you and your company are looking for. I am now ready for any questions you may have.

The conclusion of your Resume and Opening Statement is important. It lets you throw in some qualities about yourself to recap some of your major attributes. In addition, the conclusion helps smooth the transition from your resume to the interviewer's questions, rather than an awkward pause of silence where the panel members *assume* you have completed or finished speaking.

YOUR OPENING STATEMENT AND THE INTERVIEW

Unless otherwise told, be prepared to bring a printed version of your Opening Statement and your Resume to the interview. Having your Opening Statement handy will assist you in your opening remarks, but be careful not to read from it. You should already know the information. You are talking about yourself and your accomplishments, and most importantly what you have learned from them. The resume can be used as a prop to impress the panel members as to your preparedness. The resume can be offered again at the conclusion of your interview to provide the interviewer with yet another impressive reminder of you.

OBTAINING PREVIOUS ORAL INTERVIEW QUESTIONS

Attempt to gain that all important edge by obtaining previously asked oral interview questions. For those of you who have gone through the interviewing process before, hopefully you have kept an important record of the previous questions that were asked. If you haven't, or to those of you are taking an oral interview for the first time, don't panic. Most oral interview questions are different depending on the position, but you can gain some insight as to the *type* of questions that are asked. Ask the people whom you are close to who have already been promoted (the more recently promoted the better) or who currently hold similar jobs like the one you are applying for about the type of questions they were asked, and what their responses were. Ask friends or acquaintances about the type of questions they have encountered during their hiring process. Were the questions mostly related to employee problems? Did some of the questions include opinions relating to current company media events? The important thing is to not necessarily know exactly what questions were asked, but to get an idea of what *type* of questions were asked. This will assist you in the direction as to what to study or what to possibly expect.

PROBLEM SOLVING TECHNIQUES

In order to answer an interviewer's questions effectively, one must understand the problem solving techniques used in the oral interview process. As strange as this may sound we call our technique, "BUILDING A SKY LAB." When you can tell us how to build a sky lab, you will be ready for your interview. That is what we say to people when they ask us if we think they are prepared enough for their pending interview. This originated one evening when we visited a friend who was scheduled for a promotional interview the next day. The purpose behind the visit was to give him a last minute blast of encouragement and to hit him blindly with a question or two, just to see how well prepared he was. Well, he was on fire. His responses were energy driven, logically stated, and filled with all of the necessary management principles and buzz-words. His confidence and enthusiasm was evident in his face, body, and verbal responses. We felt he was ready, but there was just one more question, and then we would be sure. It was one that we knew he wasn't prepared for, yet we had no doubt he could answer, "Tell us how to build a sky lab." He smiled at us, paused briefly, and then answered the question. He applied the basic problem solving techniques, said why the various steps were important, gathered input from various components, and summed it up with a powerful closing. His response was logical, organized, sincere, and very enthusiastic. Although he knew nothing about building a sky lab, he was right on the mark in terms of organizing, planning, and managing the project. Today, we are extremely happy to report that his interview score was near perfect and today he holds a key management position.

Don't panic if you do not quite understand our technique as of yet, you will by the time you finish the book. So what does this all mean? It means that possessing a good working knowledge of the following problem solving techniques can greatly assist you when faced with a variety of both technical, management, or personnel challenges. As you go through these steps you will notice that we make managerial references. Do not let this keep you from this section, even if the position you are applying for is not management related. These steps can be applied to any job, and will be recognized, appreciated, and scored highly to those who can step back, analyze and apply them.

THE PROBLEM SOLVING STEPS

Just about every management book contains some version of standard problem solving techniques. Though each refers to the steps differently, they are all basically the same. Lets take a look at each step and break them down into simple terms.

STEP I
Identify the Problem - First, make sure you know exactly what the problem is. Whose problem is it? Can the problem be handled at your level? Or does it require decisions from a higher level, lower level, or multiple levels? Don't forget to consider the big picture as you begin to analyze the problem. The problem may be far more involved than what initially meets the eye. Is it a problem an employee is having? If so, is the problem real or imagined? Either way, it is important to treat the problem. Lastly, if it is a problem that requires you to bring it to your boss' attention, you must decide whether to speak with the boss immediately or when the problem has been resolved. Remember, don't forget the boss!

STEP II
Identify your resources - One trait that sets great managers apart from others is the ability to be resourceful. How fast can you find a telephone number to assist someone in finding a particular service or piece of equipment? As a growing manager, you should always be on the look out for a name and telephone number to a resource that could be useful in the future. One day you may need to reach out to that person and having the number on hand will speed up the process considerably, and possibly serve as a quick solution. In these tight budgetary times when we are expected to do more with less, being resourceful is one way this can be accomplished.

3-18 THE PROMOTIONAL EDGE

As you prepare for the oral interview you must compile an extensive file cabinet of resources. And we mean extensive. In plain and simple terms **you must over prepare**. You must be able to spout out a list of resources from something as minor as providing an answer to a customer's question to coordinating, planning, organizing, and staffing a department at the request of the chief executive officer. Your list of resources also pertains to your job of supervising people. Again the problem could range from referring an employee to a local community college to learn how to use a word processing program to dealing with a severely depressed subordinate who is performing poorly on the job due to marital difficulties.

STEP III

Consider your alternatives - Many times daily decisions are made relatively quick and easy. But there are others that may have far more reaching consequences that require careful analysis. The more complex decisions often have more than one way to solve them. In an oral interview for a supervisory position many candidates forget that when they are asked the questions they are expected to answer the questions from the position they are applying for. This means that you must answer the questions from the position of a supervisor, manager, or executive officer relating to the position you are applying for.

Remember, your job as a manager is to get things done through people. Don't try to do it yourself. Keep in mind that delegation is a fundamental tool of a successful manager and failure to use this tool may lower your interview score. This involves bringing employees in on the decision-making process when appropriate. Utilizing your employees (another resource) in formulating a decision has a number of benefits. Some of the most important benefits include:

- It gives employees ownership in the final outcome.
- It opens the door for more suggestions.
- It permits an easier acceptance to change.
- It increases employees' support and commitment.

STEP IV
Choose a Solution - Don't accept the most obvious solution, rather consider all of the available alternatives. Be careful not to allow the wrong person or event to dictate the speed in which your decision is made. Be sure not to rush into a decision without giving it careful thought. Weigh the circumstances such as the long-term effects of the decision, your resources, the desired results, and of course the costs involved. Lastly, do not forget to step away from your decision momentarily and look at the big picture. Many young managers often get so caught up in what is going on in their own departments that they lose sight of the world around them and how their decisions may affect other components of the company.

STEP V
Implement the Solution - As you put your plan into motion, be sure that everyone is on board. Be sure that everyone involved understands the desired outcome. When applicable, provide the theoretical goals and objectives in writing for clarity and accountability. Depending on the magnitude of the problem or project it may be necessary to have a timeline established for each component involved. A timeline will allow you to easily monitor the progress of the decision or plan as you strive toward meeting single or multiple objectives. As the decision is implemented it may be necessary to make an adjustment or two from your original plan. As a manager you must be decisive, yet flexible enough to impart change when needed. Any supervisor who fails to modify a decision when one should in the interest of many, may be viewed as too rigid and inflexible.

STEP VI
Evaluate the Outcome - It is imperative that each decision or action plan includes some form of follow-up or evaluation. This will ensure that the desired outcome is reached and identifies any modifications that may need to be made in case the problem re-occurs. Regardless if it is an employee problem or management decision, follow-up is critical in establishing credibility, future support, and in measuring the effectiveness of

your actions. Some decisions may require minimal follow-up, while others may require an in-depth written analysis of the consequences over a period of months or years.

A FEW LITTLE SECRETS

There are a few little secrets that we have found consistent among most successful oral interviewers. The first secret is one we constantly preach which is Preparation and Practice. Although this may sound elementary, many of your competitors either don't do it, or don't know how.

Secret number two is explaining WHY. We cannot stress this enough. This one separates the experienced interviewees from those that are not. Read and re-read this paragraph until it sinks in. We have consistently found that one of the differences between an average answer and an above average answer is when a candidate reveals their depth of knowledge by stating *why* they have taken the steps they did. Many candidates assume that since the assessors are obviously already experienced, then they will understand the importance or reason why you took a certain course of action. WRONG! The interviewers must feel confident that you realize the importance of the various things you say your going to do, and are not just saying them because someone told you to, or because you read it in a book. Let's take a look at some of the central topics that you should be ready to explain.

Documentation - One point to mention in almost every scenario, especially problem employee and low productivity types, is to document the problem. What is paramount for a thorough response is not just to mention the fact that the steps and the actions of everyone are documented, but to tell the interviewers WHY documentation is important. Explaining why this is important will enhance your response considerably. It shows the interviewer your depth of knowledge, and that you truly understand the importance behind each step.

So why is documentation important? It provides a permanent record of past events for which future decisions can be made. Most candidates relate the need for documentation to negative or disciplinary situations, but this is not accurate. Yes, documentation is critical to capture the steps you have taken to discipline someone or to set reachable productivity goals, but it is equally important to say that your written records will also include positive things. For example, if an employee has performed a number of exceptional projects, or has consistently shown a high level of work output, you (the supervisor) may choose to nominate the individual for a letter of recognition or an award. It is important to not only understand this, but to relay it to the board. If you are worried of insulting the panel members by telling them something they may already know, try prefacing your comments with a humble statement like, "As you ladies and gentlemen are well aware, documentation is critical to capture both negative and positive occurrences. It provides a written record that any supervisor or I can use in the future if faced with a similar decision."

Informing the chain of command - Informing the chain of command is another necessary step in most scenarios. It is not enough to just say that you would notify your chain of command, which is what the average candidate will say. You must tell the interview panel why notification is important. If you are asked a question that is going to require work from you or the people you supervise, it may become necessary to keep your chain of command informed of your actions. Try this explanation on for size. One reason is to seek their input. The best managers use all of their resources, which includes both the boss and the members of their team. Your supervisor may be able to show you a new set of ideas or provide you with a different approach to the challenge at hand. Chances are he or she has experienced a similar challenge and has learned from its outcome.

Another reason for informing the chain of command is to keep your boss abreast of the things that are going on within their department. Managers want and need to be kept informed in a timely fashion of important issues that take place within their span of control. You and your manager are responsible for carrying out certain tasks, and this cannot be done without accurate and timely information. Simple responses such as these clearly show that you understand the importance of notifying your chain of command.

Praise - Like the others, it is not enough to just say that you would praise someone. Say a few quick sentences that show you understand why praise is important. Remember, when faced with any type of question that calls for an employee to complete a task or a situation that involves motivating an employee to increase a person's productivity, it is imperative that sincere praise follows good work. Unfortunately, many supervisors get so tied up in their day to day demands that they forget the high returns praise can yield. So once you have indicated to the interview board that you would praise an employee for the work that he or she has completed, follow it up with something like this - "Praise and recognition is by far the most inexpensive tool that a supervisor has available to motivate someone. This is especially true today as managers are expected to do more with less. An employee who knows that his or her work is appreciated and acknowledged will likely repeat the exceptional behavior that brought about the recognition. Praise makes someone feel good about themselves, about you, and most tend to work harder." With just a few sentences you have convinced the board that you truly understand the importance and need for praise.

Discipline - Don't get this confused with punishment. In the business world, discipline is the manner in which order, control and efficiency are maintained (both positive and negative). Punishment is what is handed out to those who disrupt or violate the policies and regulations that were created to keep order and control. Refer to management and supervisory books for a more complete definition of both.

When posed with a question that deals with either training needs or discipline, you need to be able to say you understand the need and the difference of positive and negative discipline. So how do you express your knowledge in this area to a question? Once you have given a response that includes training or punishment, digress briefly and explain the purpose of each. For example, you have been given a scenario involving an employee who has just received his third complaint from a customer regarding his unacceptable behavior. Specifically, the employee is said to have been discourteous to customers. Your inquiry revealed that the previous complaints were handled by a former supervisor who initially gave the employee a verbal warning, and on the second occasion issued him a written counseling form. Tell the interview panel the employee's actions not only reflect poorly on the employee, but also on the company as well. Positive discipline is used when you are trying to correct a deficiency without using punishment, and normally comes in the form of training. Training can be used to correct behavior (such as employee/customer relations), or beliefs (such as cultural diversity training).

Negative discipline takes the form of punishment, which can range anywhere from a verbal reprimand to termination. Generally speaking, negative discipline will follow some form of positive discipline, unless the employee's actions were unforeseen, without warning, or strictly prohibited.

Follow-up - This is a step many experienced candidates forget to mention. It is also a step that can help to turn an average answer into a great response. So why is follow-up important? Follow-up is a different way of saying evaluation as described earlier. When a supervisor follows up on a task assigned to an employee, he is actually evaluating the employee. The supervisor should check on things such as the progress of the assignment, if it is being done correctly, the timeliness of his or her work, and how well it is being accomplished. In addition, the supervisor should recognize if the employee is in need of additional resources, and then serve as a facilitator for the employee to acquire the necessary tools to get the job done. Another critical area to mention that makes follow-up important is that without it orders, requests, and suggestions lose their importance. If a manager fails to follow-up on the simple assignments, eventually many employees will begin to give little attention to future requests or orders. What happens is that the supervisor's credibility begins to dissolve and the spoken word becomes watered down. Conversely, follow-up tends to ensure that even the slightest request receives and deserves attention. For this to occur, an employee must come to expect that the supervisor, regardless of the assignment, will be checking on its status. Through words and actions this can be accomplished with relative ease.

To avoid being redundant, remember the points we made earlier about praise and formal evaluation. Follow-up is an excellent time to tell the interview board the importance of praise, and depending on the question it may be necessary to mention the need to conduct a short or long-term formal evaluation.

Closing - We both feel that this is an extremely important part of a successful answer. If necessary, read this section several times to understand its importance. There are three types of closings that are commonly used during oral interviews. The first closing comes at the end of your opening statement. As you recall, this is when you tell the board about your education, career track, and other important points and accomplishments about yourself. The second type is your closing statement, as you prepare to leave the interview room.

The third type of closing, is one that is found at the end of each answer. As simple as it may seem, most people are unaware of this technique, or fail to use it. It is used to close each response by recapping the major points of your answer and to signal the interviewers that you are finished with your response. Using this technique provides for a powerful ending and gives you one more chance to touch briefly on a point that you may have forgotten. Without properly closing your response with some type of transitional word or phrase, often times candidates stop abruptly and leave the interviewers hanging, wondering if you are finished with your response or just blanked out.

Below are the primary benefits associated with incorporating this technique into your responses:

- The closing lets the interviewers know that your response is ending, which provides for a smooth transition. Otherwise, most candidates will answer a question and then abruptly stop. This tends to leave the panel members leaning forward in their seats, only to suddenly realize or assume that the candidate is finished.
- When used properly this technique can create a powerful closing.
- The closing allows the candidate to state new points that he or she may have forgot to mention during the body of their answer.
- The technique has a tendency to positively effect your scoring in the area of communication.

PREPARATION

Confidence is rooted in knowledge, and knowledge is rooted in preparation. You know the qualifications needed for the job, and you know the qualities and attributes that set you apart from the other candidates. Build on that, but don't overlook the research aspect for the interview. This is your chance to equip yourself with a well-rounded file cabinet of information. This is vital.

Of course it is impossible to prepare a response for every question that can be asked, but you can have a very good idea of general and often-asked questions. Remember, most questions, although different in content and structure, can be answered by using basic problem solving techniques and utilizing your interpersonal skills. Read the oral interview questions in the back of this book for an idea of what you may be asked. Many of these are actual oral interview questions that have been asked during the promotional and hiring phase of various companies.

You will notice that once you get accustomed and comfortable with the questions, many are not that much different from one another. They all require basic problem-solving skills. Keep in mind when formulating your responses and Opening Statement to stay away from trite statements found in other interview books, such as, *"I'm a people person."* Although this statement may be true about you, you need to convey the real meaning behind the response in a more original, less cliché way. With this in mind, we ask you, what is a *people person?* You may have an explanation in mind, but you need to convey those thoughts. Offer an example that illustrates *how* you acted as a *people person*. Maybe it was simply listening to other employees when they had a problem or offering them guidance and training in order for them to reach their potential. Your interviewer will be more impressed if you avoid these overused statements and come up with more original phrases. This is where the use of the Power Words (Chapter 4) come into play in formulating Power Phrases to convey your true thoughts and ideas.

FORMULATING QUESTIONS AND ANSWERS

In a broad sense, come up with as many questions and scenarios as you can based upon the position you are seeking. To do this, refer to the duties and responsibilities of the job. Consider the primary and secondary functions of your sought after position when formulating your questions. Also consider current events, your strengths and weaknesses, and lastly and most importantly, the five assessed areas described in the assessment chapter when formulating your responses.

The idea behind creating questions, scenarios, and responses is two-fold. First, they will help you realize, maybe for the first time, the problems and challenges you will face in the position you are applying for. In addition, creating scenarios, questions, and responses will help prepare you to *think* and respond intelligently.

Secondly, they will challenge your intellectual, technical and conceptual capabilities (depending on the type of job) while building on your catalog of ideas, solutions to problems, examples and resources. With writing out your responses and saying them aloud, you will improve your delivery, communication skills, and sharpen your ability to think and act as the position requires. It will also improve the methodology involved in solving and analyzing the problems you will face as an employee or supervisor.

By formulating answers to possible questions and scenarios, you are taking the most random selection process and controlling the outcome. That's right, we said you are in control. It is a very simple process that has a tremendous effect on your confidence. Once you are fully prepared, as odd as it may sound, you will have the desire of *wanting* to be interviewed. You will have the confidence that there will not be a question an interviewer can possibly throw at you without you being able to answer with authority. The following is a brief outline of the interviewing techniques that you can use. We will describe some of these studying techniques in more detail in the next couple of pages.

- **Formulate possible interview questions** - the questions should stem from your experiences, skills, accomplishments, and how you deal with various organizational problems.

- **Customize the answers to your style** - the answers should stem from your vocabulary and manner of speaking. Use some of the Power Words found in the proceeding chapter to help formulate your responses and phrases. Remember your conceptual skills. Look at the Big Picture. If you have a problem, not only is it necessary to solve the immediate problem, but it is equally important to find the *underlying* cause of the problem. For example, if a subordinate's performance has deteriorated it is important that you correct the immediate problem, but it is even more important to discover the underlying cause of the problem. Were there marital difficulties or possibly a death in the family that was causing problems and stress in the employee's life? As a manager, it is your responsibility to help the subordinate. This is where your interpersonal skills as a supervisor will show through. Talk with the subordinate, recommend counseling, or refer the subordinate to an employee assistance program. Whatever the case, the employee is valuable. Remember, leaders get work accomplished through their subordinates.

- **You are the best person for the job** - you must convey the fact that you are the person the company is looking for, the one with commitment, desire, and dedication.

- **Don't overlook *follow-up*** - when you make decisions or recommendations as a supervisor, you must conduct appropriate follow-up to determine if the problem has been resolved.

- **Record your responses** (Mock Oral Interview) - one of the most useful tools in preparing for the oral interview is the use of a video camera to help critique yourself. At first this will seem awkward, but don't let this stand in your way. Soon you will be used to performing in front of a camera and in front of friends, all of which will seem more stressful than talking to a panel of strangers. Practicing under these conditions will greatly enhance your demeanor and delivery on the Big Day. It is important to simulate an interview. Watch the way you deliver your responses and your mannerisms. Also valuable is a cassette recorder. The cassette tapes can be played on a portable cassette player while you are driving in your car, jogging, or whatever. Repetition is the best source for exercising your gray-matter. Eventually your responses will filter into your subconscious, and thus, your answers will become second nature.

- **Rehearse, Rehearse, Rehearse** - play your taped video or audio recordings over and over again. Pay attention to your mannerisms and remember what was said earlier about using gestures. Use your hands to drive home a point if that is your style, but be careful not to over do it. Facial expressions and body movement can also play an important role. Leaning slightly forward in your chair can be an effective way to drive home a point. Smile occasionally, and remember to maintain eye contact. It is not just what you say, but *how* you state your responses. Your nonverbal communication skills are invaluable. It is important *how* you come across or convey your ideas during the oral interview.

- **Repeat the process** - edit and revise your responses as you polish your delivery. Turn off the music and make use of your spare time by playing the recordings when you are driving or jogging. Don't just think about or listen to your responses, but say your responses aloud. Again, this reinforces what your brain is hearing.

GETTING READY

Think about the last time you took part in something and were successful. Maybe it was a sport you played or a time when you gave guidance to one of your children. You were playing a role at the time. In the sport you played, you practiced the techniques needed to win. In the parenting scenario you thought out the problem and solved it with your interpersonal skills. You certainly played a different role as a parent than you did as a participant in a sport, but in each case you strived for a successful conclusion.

Understand the game and the role you must play in the oral interview process. Most interviewing processes do *not* focus on the importance of your qualifications, but focus on your personality as the biggest asset to success in any interviewing situation. If job qualifications were the best or only factors considered in getting hired, there would be no need for an interview.

How you look, dress, communicate your ideas, how well you listen, and how much enthusiasm you convey all make up your personality. Even the shyest people can take charge of a situation given the right set of circumstances. On the flip side, some of the most boisterous people we know have a sensitive side. For better or worse, you do not have to change your personality. You just simply have to present the best and most salable side of your personality depending on the situation.

PRACTICE, PRACTICE, PRACTICE

As we stated before, practice your delivery in front of a video camera. If you cannot beg or borrow one, purchase an inexpensive audiocassette recorder and practice in front of a mirror. Some people feel that this is extreme, but we have found this to be extremely beneficial. No one has to ever see or hear the recordings. This benefit is for only you to see and hear. You will be the judge of your delivery and responses. Believe us, you will be much more critical of yourself than anyone else will ever be. Many people have little nervous habits that they are unaware of. For that reason, you may want to try a few practice interviews. What do you do unconsciously when speaking to people? Do you pick your nails? Do you play with your hair? Watch for any such undesirable habits, and then find ways to avoid them.

Select a question you think may be asked during the oral interview and formulate a response to the question. Turn on the camera and give your best delivery. Now play back the tape. Do you like what you see? Are you articulate? Would you consider hiring or promoting this person? Does this person inspire enthusiasm and confidence? At first you will probably be a little disappointed in your delivery, but don't despair. You will improve. Remember, you must first learn how to walk before you can run a marathon.

Practice assuming a role as a confident interviewee and ham it up a bit. Think about how a confident person thinks, acts, their mannerisms, and the words they use. Think of a person you admire and shape their mannerisms to fit your personality, but don't try to be someone else, use your own personality. Okay. Now start taping.

When you play back the tape, you may be pleasantly surprised. Do you sound and look more confident? Do you recognize some of the more confident things you did more than others? Chances are you will.

One more thing, write down some of the qualities and ideas you believe you possess. Say a couple of statements to back up your thoughts. Tape yourself and verbalize your qualities as a good employee or manager. Now, play back the tape and evaluate your response. How did you do? If you were the interviewer how would you judge yourself? More importantly, what might you do or say to make yourself more believable?

Practicing this way does wonders for your confidence and delivery, but you must practice and rehearse your part. Take your time and be as articulate as possible. The good thing about this technique is that you can adjust and make changes consistent with your personality. Let your personality shine through. Remember to project confidence and enthusiasm, and you will be well on your way to getting hired or promoted.

Preparation -
"The man who is prepared has his battle half fought."
Migual De Cervantes (1547-1616) Spanish Playwright

3-32 THE PROMOTIONAL EDGE

COMMENTS/NOTES

Power Words   4

Effective communication is essential to be successful in an oral interview and choosing the right words or phase is essential in effective communication. The following Power Words will be useful in the development of your answers to an interviewer's questions. The words are interchangeable with one another and by no means limited to the words in this book. Check out a thesaurus and some management books to come up with some of your own. Using the words listed will increase your vocabulary and enhance your delivery. It is a good idea when designing your Opening and Closing remarks to plug in a few Power Words. Power Words when combined together create catchy little phrases that can be used to place emphasis on a response. The following are just a few.

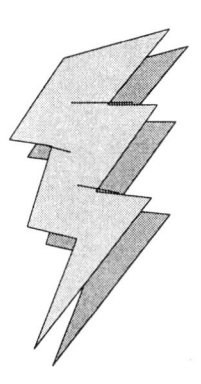

A

accelerated	accentuated	accurate	acquired
accomplished	achieved	actively	adapted
addressed	administered	advised	aided
allocated	alluring	ambitious	analytical
appraised	approved	arbitrated	arranged
articulate	assembled	asserted	assessed
asset	assisted	attained	audited
augmented	authored	authorized	awarded

B

balanced	benefited	boosted	built
brainstormed	briefed	broadened	budgeted

4-2 THE PROMOTIONAL EDGE

C

calculated	capable	capitalize	cataloged
centralized	challenging	chaired	charismatic
clarified	classified	coached	cohesive
collaborated	commanded	communicate	competent
compiled	completed	composed	concise
comprehensive	computed	conceived	conducted
conceptualized	confident	conscientious	considerable
consistent	consolidated	constructive	consulted
contracted	contributed	cooperative	coordinated
counseled	courage	created	cultivated

D

decisive	dedicated	delegated	drafted
demonstrated	dependable	designed	detected
determined	developed	devised	devoted
differentiate	diligent	diplomatic	directed
discussed	designed	displayed	dynamic
disseminated	distinctive	distributed	documented

E

eager	edited	educated	effective
elected	eliminated	emulated	enabled
enacted	encouraged	enforced	enlisted
encompassed	energetic	enhance	enlighten
ensured	enthusiastic	envisioned	equated
established	evaluated	examined	exceeded
excellent	extraordinary	exceptional	executed
expanded	explained	expressed	excelled

F

faithful	facilitated	fair	familiarized
financed	flexible	focused	follow-up
foresees	formulated	fostered	founded

POWER WORDS 4-3

G

| gained | gathered | generated | genuine |
| governed | graduated | growth | guided |

H

| handled | hands-on | harmonious | headed |
| helped | helpful | hired | honest |

I

identified	imaginative	immense	implemented
impressive	improved	incorporated	increased
independent	industrious	informative	ingenious
initiated	innovative	inspected	inspired
installed	instilled	instructed	insured
interacted	invented	investigated	involved

L

| launched | lectured | logical | led |

M

maintained	managed	marketed	maximum
meaningful	mediated	mentored	moderated
modernized	modified	monitored	motivated

O

objective	observant	obtained	operated
open-minded	opportunistic	optimal	optimistic
orderly	organized	originated	outstanding

P

patterned	participated	patient	perceptive
perfected	performed	persuaded	persuasive
pioneered	planned	pleasant	poised
polished	positive	powerful	practical
precise	prepared	presented	presided
prioritized	processed	procured	produced
productive	professional	proficient	progressive
prominent	promoted	proper	proposed
provided	prudent	publicized	published

Q

qualified	quality	quantified	query

R

raised	rational	realistic	reconciled
recommended	recognized	recorded	recruited
reduced	regulated	reinforced	related
reliable	remodeled	reorganized	repositioned
represented	researched	reported	responded
reshaped	restructured	resourceful	resolved
respectful	responsive	revised	reviewed
revolutionized	revitalized	routed	revamped

S

scheduled	screened	secured	selected
significant	simplified	sincere	solved
spearheaded	sponsored	staged	started
strengthened	stimulated	streamlined	structured
successful	summarized	superior	supervised
supplemented	supportive	surveyed	systematic

T

tactful	targeted	taught	tested
thankful	trained	translated	trustworthy
truthful	theorized	translated	tutored

U

| ultimate | understood | updated | utilized |

V

| valuable | verified | versatile | vitalized |

That's our list of Power Words we have used in the past. With a little thought you may come up with some of your own Power Words that you may find beneficial. Many of the words are ones that you already know. Going over them frequently and using them in your responses will quickly increase your vocabulary.

Authors of best selling novels use words that are well thought out to add impact to their stories and to keep the reader turning the page. Keep your one-liners short, clear, concise, and to the point, and your responses will begin to flow smoothly. Convey your enthusiasm in all of your Power Phrases. Blend in the Power Words to your own unique style to drive home your point or thoughts. Keep the interviewers listening to your every word, keep them wanting to turn the page.

Listed on the following pages are some Power Words combined together to create Power Phrases you can use when responding to oral interview questions. Notice the impact these words make when combined together.

- "Assisted in the planning phase... to increase productivity."
- "Restructured the auditing system... increased accuracy."
- "Minimized staffing... while maintaining efficiency."

- "Contributed expertise... gained additional knowledge."
- "Represented the company... improved communication."
- "Modified the old concept of... by innovative training."
- "Allocated resources... to a fund volunteer organization."
- "Instituted procedures... governed unionization."
- "Spearheaded efforts... sponsored a bill."
- "Mediated conflicts... to negotiate a contract."
- "Briefed management... apprised of recent development."
- "Compiled manuscripts... edited the documentation."
- "Interviewed students... gathered data."
- "Devised a marketing plan... revolutionized sales."
- "Conceptualized program... established long-term objectives."
- "Revised company goals... to improve targeted objectives."
- "Authored a training module... to improve employee performance."
- "Initiated problem-solving techniques... to heighten management effectiveness."
- "Selected to represent the department... to improve overall coordination between companies."

Learning -
"What we have to learn to do, we learn by doing."
Aristole (384-322 BC) Greek Philosopher

The Critique   5

On the proceeding pages are some typical oral interview questions. We have performed a very *basic* breakdown of the questions and have analyzed some typical and not-so-typical responses to the questions. Usually, there are no "right" or "wrong" answers in most oral interviewing processes, however, the way one responds and the content of the responses can make all the difference. We have critiqued and analyzed each question and answer to give you an understanding of why some answers are scored poorly, in addition to a topical analysis of what most interviewers are looking for in response to oral interview questions.

Question 1: As a sales representative, how do you plan on establishing yearly goals and objectives for your department?

Analysis: This question tests the applicant's communication, motivational, and management skills. This question can easily be answered with three or four sentences, but it will be a shallow response at best. This is a great chance to show your stuff, to show your enthusiasm, skills, and maybe even plug in a past experience relating to the same type of issue. A good sales representative can become a great sales representative when he or she knows how to use all of the resources available.

Dead-in-the-Water Answer: "Since I would be new to the company, it wouldn't be right for me to just dive in and start setting department goals and objectives. It wouldn't be fair to the company. Instead, I would call a meeting with my boss and ask him or her what goals and objectives they would like for me to implement. This way I would know exactly what my boss wanted and there would be no misunderstandings as to what needs to be accomplished for the year."

Critique: At first glance this answer may appear to be adequate, but it severely misses the mark. In fact, it indicates laziness or incompetence on the employee's part. The response lacks motivation and creativity with a heavy reliance on the boss to name a few. You wonder if the employee even brought a pen to the meeting, or did he/she have to borrow one from the boss.

Winning Response: (Pause first and think of what the question is asking. Remember, a quick response can indicate that your decision and actions are made with little thought. It may also show your immaturity as a leader.) Now let's look at a better response.

"As a new employee, first it would be necessary for me to closely examine the company's guidelines, to ensure that proper protocol is followed. Next, I would review the previous year's goals and objectives and see how they were evaluated and what the results were. Based on the results and my own ideas, I would rough out some goals and objectives of my own. After this, I would arrange a department meeting to solicit the input of the employees regarding setting reachable goals and objectives for the coming year. This participative management style allows employees to have some ownership in the policy of the company, builds on their trust with management, and allows the department to work as a more cohesive team."

"Next, I would check with the other supervisors who interact with my department to see if similar goals exist, or have been attempted in the past. I would then seek out their input and advice. As you ladies and gentlemen know, it is important to learn what has worked, failed, and why. Without such research, time and money may be wasted. On the other hand, more money for the company could be saved. It would then be necessary to talk with my supervisor to be sure that my expectations were in line with his and the company's policies, goals, and objectives. As a sales representative, I must realize that the actions of my department must be consistent with the company's primary mission."

Documentation – "Once I (in conjunction with any other department supervisors if applicable) have established reachable and measurable goals, I would prepare a draft of these goals for my supervisor to review. This will help to ensure that we are all on the same page before the goals are made final and given to the department members. Once we reach an agreement on these expectations, each member of the department would be provided with a copy, which they would be expected to sign. This will provide any future supervisor, or me, with written documentation as to what is expected of each employee for accountability purposes. Documentation is important because it provides for a written reference from which future decisions of all types can be made involving employees, the department, and a small part of the entire company."

Follow-up and praise – "Once the goals have been reached and are in place, I would set up a system where I could closely monitor, measure, and report the department's productivity each month to my supervisor. This will provide me with a tool to follow-up and measure our success. A measuring device such as this would be useful when preparing Planning & Performance Evaluations, when counseling or disciplining employees for lack of productivity, or for rewarding employees when their accomplishments far exceed the standard. Which brings me to an important point. My job is to also find ways to motivate employees to reach those goals. I mention this because praise is the cheapest form of motivation, yet one of the most effective motivators a supervisor has available and should be used to get the most out of each employee. Praise makes a person feel good about themselves and their work. People have a tendency to work harder when they know their work is recognized and appreciated. This is important in this day and age when managers are expected to do more with less."

Informing the chain of command – "Of course my supervisor would be kept appraised of the department's productivity and its effect on employee morale. It is important that my boss be kept informed of this information because as a supervisor he is tasked with overseeing their actions at a higher level. Knowing this type of information permits him or her to be better equipped to make future decisions concerning the department."

Closing – "If I could put it all together in a few words, let me emphasize that when establishing productivity goals, it is important to seek out the opinions and advice at various levels. In this case I have sought out advice from those responsible for carrying out the tasks and other inter-related department members as well as management personnel. I'm sure you will agree that good managers often become great managers when they learn to see beyond their own opinions and seek out the advice and direction from the resources around them."

Critique: Your efforts in determining the department's future goals will surely be impressive. Instead of taking a passive role as a new employee, you researched, investigated, and approached your boss prepared with ideas and a tentative plan rather than with a blank sheet of paper. Your actions are indicative of a highly motivated, get-it-done type of employee who possess strong organizational and leadership skills. In the closing paragraph, we announced to the board that the answer was ending which provided a smooth transition. We followed with a few short sentences that highlighted a portion of the answer, and ended with a powerful one-liner about the importance of being resourceful. In less than thirty seconds we brought our answer to a smooth and effective close.

THE CRITIQUE 5-5

In the remaining questions, we have purposely left a place for you to plug in and modify your own custom answers.

Question 2: **In what ways have you been a leader?**
Analysis: The leadership potential of an employee is one of the most valuable traits in any organization. A candidate's proper response to this question can go a long way in the hiring or promotional oral interview process. The interviewer is looking for examples of professional development and judging your future potential. This is a golden opportunity to sell yourself, so don't sell yourself short.

Dead-in-the-Water Answer: "Some people are just born natural leaders, and I think I'm one of them. Leadership is something you can't teach. Either you got it or you don't."
Critique: Never mind the fact that the response is too brief or the candidate's head won't be able to fit through the doorway on the way out, but this particular answer doesn't say anything about the person. It also implies that this person will not contribute to the leadership potential of others under his or her supervision, nor does the candidate have a remote grasp of what the management abilities and qualities of a leader truly are.

Winning Answer: (State some of the tasks you have performed. More importantly, state what you have learned from them, and then end your response with something like the following.) "I have been entrusted in the position of a supervisor on several occasions, and I have been responsible for seeing tasks performed properly with successful outcomes. Each time I have taken the job seriously, and found it helps generate the desire in me to help others even more. I find myself observing others with management potential and have been able to help foster their development through training and simply taking the time to talk about my experiences. I also find it helps me hone my skills and reach my potential as an effective supervisor. The real challenge for me, and self-satisfaction, is helping others to reach their potential (finish with a powerful closing)."

Critique: This response indicates the candidate has a successful track record by stating past performance and what he or she has learned from the experience. More importantly, it shows that the candidate has an understanding of what makes a good supervisor, thus suggesting the candidate is speaking from experience. (Notice the use of the Power Words: management, supervisor, entrusted, responsible, performed, development, training, experience, effective, challenge, self-satisfaction, potential.)

Question 3: What is your greatest strength and weakness as a supervisor?

Analysis: First, the question has two parts. The biggest danger to this question is stating something negative about yourself. This is a direct invitation to place your head on the chopping block, so don't fall into the trap. Many candidates will not expound on their strengths, and will only concentrate on their weaknesses making excuses for any deficiencies. It is important to remember to present your responses not only to inform the assessors about yourself, but to also express your understanding of management principles and your capability to see the Big Picture.

Dead-in-the-Water Answer: "In terms of strength, I'm pretty much knowledgeable about all facets of management in the positions I've held. I think my skills are second to none. As far as any weaknesses, I will usually get bored if I'm not doing something to occupy my time."

Critique: The biggest problem with this response is that the candidate hasn't told the interviewers anything about his strengths. The candidate assumes the interviewers understand what he is talking about and presents no examples to illustrate his conclusion. The response to the second part of the answer implies that he has no initiative. It hints that the candidate must be given a task from others to keep him busy, rather than doing something on his own. If he cannot motivate himself as a leader, how will he be able to motivate others?

Winning Answer: "In terms of strengths, I find my organizational skills to be an asset to me and to others as well. (Demonstrate your positive personality traits. Give examples, isolate your high points, explain what you learned from them as well as what others have learned from them. Did the company benefit from your expertise? How? Why?) My greatest weakness is that I have little patience for laziness. I have recognized this weakness and have found that if I take the time to help others in seeing their potential, it helps motivate the person in wanting to learn and do more (finish with a powerful closing)."

Critique: This response does two things. It clearly identifies the candidate's strengths and his conceptual knowledge. The candidate's weakness can easily be perceived as a strength, and also shows the candidate's ability to overcome his weakness through problem solving and management principles while showing his interpersonal skills.

Question 4: Why do you feel you can be successful in this position?

Analysis: A fairly open-ended question. With this question, the interviewer is not so much interested in examples of your past successes, but wants to know what makes you tick. This question serves as an opportunity for the candidate to demonstrate his value, enthusiasm, and talents. The candidate's response will give the assessors information about the candidate's drive, conceptual knowledge, and self-confidence.

Dead-in-the-Water Answer: "I don't know, I guess I'm pretty good at most things I do. If I get hired I know I could do the job. I've always been successful in the past in most things I have done, if I set my mind to it."

Critique: The answer is lacking in several ways. First and foremost the language is extremely weak. Never use phrases such as; "I don't know," when your talking about yourself. If you don't know, then who does? The term, "pretty good" does nothing for the candidate and shows a lack of assertiveness and enthusiasm. The candidate also suggests that he or she is lacking in some abilities to be successful in everything he or she does. Finally, the terminology or statement, "if I set my mind to it," implies the candidate will only be successful when he or she feels like it.

Winning Answer: "As I stated previously in my resume, the tasks I have initiated and have been asked to perform, such as (list prior accomplishments, programs, and management tasks), have all met with a successful conclusion. I have learned from my experiences and have gained a tremendous amount of insight in my capabilities as a manager and supervisor (state your drive, determination, conceptual knowledge, and what you have learned; problem-solving abilities, organizational skills, and the desire to do the job). I have the requisite skills to succeed in this position and look forward to the challenges this position will offer (finish with a powerful closing)."

Critique: This is a strong response. It tells the interviewer the candidate has both the skills and the knowledge to do the job. The candidate's illustration of prior tasks performed and accomplishments reinforces the candidate's statement. The candidate expresses self-confidence in his or her abilities and shows enthusiasm toward the job. Lastly, the candidate shows that he or she has learned from experience and accepts the responsibility of the position as a positive challenge.

POSITIVE TRAITS

The assessors will ask you probing questions that are designed to test your confidence, poise, personality traits, and analytical thinking. The positive traits you express will help distinguish you from the other candidates. These traits will label you as reliable, loyal, dedicated, and a candidate for professional growth. When formulating your responses to the oral interview questions, remember that the assessors are looking for certain tangible assets and personality traits. Building those assets and traits into your responses will greatly assist you in achieving your goal. As the oral interview unfolds, formulate your responses to meet each trait. We have listed the Top Ten traits, in no particular order, that most assessors are looking for in an employee:

- **Analysis** - problem solving
- **Drive** - a desire to get things accomplished
- **Motivation** - enthusiasm for the job
- **Determination** - not backing away from a problem
- **Confidence** - well poised, open, friendly, and honest
- **Reliability** - dependable, ensures the tasks are accomplished
- **Integrity** - taking responsibility for your actions
- **Pride** - in your profession
- **Dedication** - whatever time and effort it takes to accomplish your goals
- **Efficiency** - performing tasks without wasting time, energy, or resources

Success-
"Success is a matter of luck. Ask any failure."
Earl Wilson - American Columnist

COMMENTS/NOTES

Body Language 6

Although language is the main device through which we communicate, nonverbal clues often tell more. Since the beginning of time, humans have relied heavily on gathering information visually. We have been sending and receiving nonverbal signals to one another since man first appeared as a species. Body language is the first method of communication we learn. A mother is well aware whether her child is upset or happy without the child ever speaking a word. As we develop into adulthood these unspoken signals are still sent and received. Try this experiment, turn on the television and turn down the volume when watching the end of a sporting event. Can you tell who are the victors? Sure you can. The winners are smiling, shoulders square, and their heads are held high. The losers are tight-lipped with their heads bowed in defeat.

CONTROLING NONVERBAL MESSAGES

The way we react to a situation will send nonverbal messages. When our body language complements our verbal statements, our message can gain a tremendous positive impact. Likewise, when our body language contradicts what we say, our verbal message will be distorted. Learning to control your body language during the interview process will greatly increase your chances of getting hired or promoted. A warm and firm handshake before and after an interview, coupled with a smile and direct eye contact, shows self-confidence which creates a lasting positive impression. It is important to realize the significance attached to both language and actions.

The old adage that our actions speak louder than words still holds true today. Facial expressions, body posture, and your personal demeanor contribute as much to verbal communication as the spoken word.

Appropriate control and the effective use of body language will greatly enhance the positive traits of your personality. Erect posture with control over body movements will convey confidence and a positive mental attitude. Everything about you is observed and evaluated during the interview process, not only your responses to an interviewer's questions but your dress, facial expressions, posture, and gestures as well. Listed below are some suggestions to help you succeed. Many of the suggestions may seem simplistic, but you would be surprised how many people forget about them during the oral interview. Don't be one of them.

Facial Expressions
While all parts of our bodies are capable of sending nonverbal messages, our face is under the most scrutiny especially during the oral interview process. Interviewers will establish eye contact with you the moment you walk into the interview room, thus whatever facial message you send during the oral interview will be evaluated. Tight smiles and tense facial muscles communicate apprehensiveness and uncertainty. Little eye contact or eyes darting downward bespeak of intimidation and doubt. Be mindful of the nonverbal messages you send.

The Eyes
When you establish eye contact with an interviewer you create a bond of communication. Looking at someone shows interest. This nonverbal body language can be one of the most important aspects of the interview. Looking away, shifting your eyes repeatedly, or closing your eyes during an interview will send the wrong message when you speak. The one who never looks at the interviewer in the eyes will appear to have something to hide. Your goal is to have a calm, non-threatening gaze. Look at the interviewer while you speak and maintain eye contact, but be careful not to stare. Create a mental triangle with the interviewer's face incorporating the interviewer's eyes and mouth. If you are

being interviewed by more than one person at a time, break your gaze and speak to both of the interviewers not just the one who asked a question, but don't break your gaze too abruptly. This will allow you to leave the impression that you are attentive. Eyebrows send nonverbal messages as well. Wrinkled brows can send a negative message about our ability to handle challenges or stress. Raised eyebrows, however, will send a message that we are interested and enthusiastic.

The Head

The slow nodding of the head emphasizes interest and helps validate comments. Rapidly nodding your head can show impatience and may give the interviewer the impression you want to interrupt the conversation. However, if you can get the interviewers to nod their heads with you during your responses, this is a positive sign and you will have succeeded where most will fail.

The Mouth

Your smile is one of the most positive nonverbal messages you can send. Many interviewees are under the misconception that an oral interview mirrors a military tribunal where the candidate must be rigid and expressionless during the entire interview process. Nothing could be further from the truth. Offer a confident, friendly smile when the circumstances dictate, but avoid grinning during the interview as this will communicate insincerity or that you're a couple of bricks short of a full load. A relaxed, pleasant, sincere smile goes a long way. A friendly person is perceived as an agreeable person, and everyone likes to work with agreeable, friendly people. Be aware of the negative nonverbal clues regarding the mouth. Gnawing or licking your lips frequently will send a negative message.

Miscellaneous

During an interview you should sit tall, shoulders back, and head erect. Erect posture will convey a confident attitude. Attempt to reinforce the positive signals your interviewer sends to you. This is commonly called "mirroring." If your interviewer starts to laugh, you too should *subtly* laugh along with the interviewer. If the interviewer leans forward in his chair, wait a minute or two and lean slightly forward in your chair. Look for the positive signals and go with it. The mirroring technique is part of the *bonding process* (explained in more detail in later chapters). The bonding process is a psychological emotion that will help you align yourself with the interviewer.

Be careful of some of the other negative nonverbal clues. Pulling at your socks or repeatedly clearing your throat during the interview will show your nervousness. Pulling at your collar and picking lint from your clothing, whether real or imaginary, can also send a negative message that will display your inability to handle stressful situations. Avoid at all cost any other nervous tics that will leave the interviewer with a negative impression of you.

Listed below is a checklist of a few *do's* and *don'ts* to consider during an interview.

Here are a few positive nonverbal messages to remember:
☺ Smile
☺ Walk slowly and deliberately
☺ Relax
☺ Sit well back in the chair
☺ Maintain an alert posture
☺ Maintain eye contact

Below are a few negative nonverbal messages you should avoid at all cost:
☹ Don't jingle change in your pocket
☹ Don't fold your arms across your chest
☹ Don't sit with your arms or legs too far apart
☹ Don't offer a limp handshake
☹ Don't fidget
☹ Don't slump in your seat
☹ Don't slouch your shoulders
☹ Don't tap your feet
☹ Don't tap your fingers

- ☹ Don't twirl or play with your hair
- ☹ Don't shift in your chair
- ☹ Don't start adjusting your tie
- ☹ Don't look at your watch

It is not what you say, but *how* you say it. Just as you interpret body language of others, you too leave an impression on those you meet. Job interviews bring out insecurities in all of us. However, the more positive messages you give an interviewer, the more you will be perceived as the best candidate for the job. Positive signals reinforce one another. Understanding and controlling your body language will greatly increase your chances of success. Positive body language will create a positive impression and show others you have confidence in yourself.

Knowledge -
"Knowledge is the antidote to fear."
Ralph Waldo Emerson (1803-1882) American Philosopher

COMMENTS/NOTES

The Assessment 7

ORAL INTERVIEW PARAMETERS

The oral interview parameters vary as much as the interviews themselves. However, most oral interviews normally last, on average, approximately thirty minutes. Thirty minutes for an interviewer or a panel of interviewers to assess you on your ability to do the job, and whether or not you should be hired. During the interview a series of questions will be asked which you will be expected to answer. It is important for you to not ramble on about one particular question during your interview, but rather give complete and concise answers to all of the oral interview questions.

BE YOURSELF, BE YOURSELF, BE YOURSELF

Contrary to what some authors of interview books suggest, one of the most important pieces of advice anyone can offer as you prepare for the oral interview and sit down at the table before the interviewer is to BE YOURSELF. Don't try to emulate someone else you admire. Don't try to be older or younger than you are. Don't use words you don't understand or have difficulty pronouncing. Don't try to talk without using your hands when you normally do to stress a point. All of these things will only create a distraction for you causing you to concentrate on what you are doing physically, rather than concentrating mentally on what you have toiled over, prepared for, and researched. Your ability to concentrate on your answers to an interviewer's questions will be impeded if you are overwhelmed by playing an imaginary role. Put your best foot forward and be yourself. You got this far on your own.

HOW DOES THE INTERVIEWER FEEL?

Let's learn a little about those who are rating us. Contrary to what many may think, the person interviewing you will usually be anxious and excited for you. Remember, they had to go through the same experiences you will be going through during the oral interview process. In fact, they too will be a little nervous about their role as an assessor, especially at the beginning of the oral interview. For the most part they are in unfamiliar territory. Most companies do not train their personnel extensively as interviewers. What's good about this is that you can put them at ease with your demeanor and attitude. But what exactly is going through their minds? The most useful and reassuring fact we can give you right now is that the interviewer who is conducting the interview wants you to succeed. They want you to do the best you can possibly do. It's enjoyable for an interviewer to hear a good interview. Remember, their job is to establish an eligibility list of good, qualified potential employees. They will be most satisfied if they select candidates who will succeed in the positions they are interviewing for.

WHAT IS THE PURPOSE OF FOLLOW-UP QUESTIONS?

During the questioning process you may feel an interviewer may be trying to seek out your hidden weaknesses, to confuse you or keep you on the defensive by asking follow-up questions. This is usually not the case. By pushing points in some detail, an interviewer learns something about your understanding of principles, attitude and poise, your ability to think and express yourself clearly, your judgment, your convictions, and a little something about your temperament.

Often times, follow-up or probing questions are asked in an attempt to have the interviewee hit on a point that the interviewer is confident the job candidate may know, but has missed. Remember, the interviewers want you to succeed, so don't worry when a follow-up question is asked.

JOB RELATED SKILLS

Interviewers ask questions to find out about your skills. Interviewers want to know if your skills qualify you for a certain job. They are looking for someone with the right skills and qualifications, and the ability to learn the necessary new skills. Out of the countless questions an interviewer may ask you, there is really only one interview question and it underlies all others. Don't be bothered by the complexity of a question, and don't let an interviewer's sophistication, or lack of it, throw you off. Every question asked of you in an interview is based upon the company's concern of whether you can do the job. You must guarantee yourself a high quality reply to the underlying question. That means your proof must be offered in a framework of preparation.

Job related skills are the basic work skills needed to do a good job. Employers ask about job related skills during the interview so they can determine whether or not applicants have a working knowledge of the job. It is important that you make several different skill statements during an interview. You must do this to let the interviewer know you are the best person for the position you seek. Make your statements positive. Tell the interviewer how you used your skills in former positions. Examples from past experiences must be introduced to reassure the interviewer. Interviewers would rather have you simply transfer already demonstrated abilities to their company, rather than train you in every aspect of a position.

MOST COMMONLY ASSESSED AREAS

The areas most commonly assessed during oral interviews are relatively the same in most interviews you will encounter. Sometimes the criteria may be worded slightly different, but the content generally remains the same in most interviews. The four most commonly rated areas of an oral interview are outlined on the following page.

PERSONAL PROFILE	BUSINESS PROFILE
Drive	Budgeting
Motivation	Organizing
Enthusiasm	Staffing
Determination	Planning
Pride	Directing
Confidence	Coordinating
Dedication	Efficiency
Integrity	Discipline

PROFESSIONAL SKILLS	ACHIEVEMENTS
Work Experience	Education
Communication Skills	Training
Listening Skills	Honors
Interpersonal Skills	Awards
Assume Responsibility	Accomplishments
Management Skills	

To help better understand each of the criteria, we have included various definitions as offered by several resources. With these you can see, possibly for the first time, what the interviewers are looking for in their employees.

PERSONAL PROFILE – the interviewer will search for these traits in your answers to specific job performance questions. The following words are the admired traits employers are seeking. They are your ticket to a successful interview.

- *Drive* – goal oriented. A desired to get things done.
- *Motivation* – accepts challenges and has enthusiasm toward the job.
- *Enthusiasm* – always willing to give that extra effort. Energetic. Morale oriented.
- *Determination* – determined to get things done and works within deadlines.
- *Pride* – always promotes personal best in whatever the task performed and loyalty to the company.
- *Confidence* – self-assurance and self-control in their abilities.

- *Dedication* – does whatever is needed to accomplish company projects and goals.
- *Integrity* – open and honest, makes decisions in the best interest of the company.

BUSINESS PROFILE – this dimension is an opportunity to demonstrate the different ways you can contribute to the company, and gives the interviewer an understanding of your knowledge of key management terminology.

- *Budgeting* – working within a company's monetary and managing resources.
- *Organizing* – efficiently and effectively manages tasks or projects without wasted time and effort.
- *Staffing* – the amount of manpower to effectively and efficiently get the job done.
- *Planning* – problem-solving through effective means.
- *Directing* – understanding the receiving and conveying of directives via verbal or written communication.
- *Coordinating* – joint projects/tasks and managing the efforts between two or more departments within a company.
- *Efficiency* – how well you manage your time, effort, and resources.
- *Discipline* – can you follow company rules and regulations, and do you have an understanding of the difference between positive (training) and negative (punitive) discipline.

PROFESSIONAL SKILLS – companies seek employees who respect their profession. Projecting these professional dimensions will establish you as a confident and reliable professional.

- *Work Experience* – this will include a list of jobs or positions you have held in chronological order. Most importantly, it should not be just a list of your duties and responsibilities, but rather what you have learned from your experiences and how you will relate those experiences to the present position you are seeking.
- *Communication/Listening Skills* - this will include the logic, reasoning, and organization of your responses. Overall, the

interviewer will judge you on your ability to convey your thoughts and ideas. Are your responses well thought out, organized, and focused? Do you express opinions and facts in a comprehensive manner? Are your responses informative and pertinent? Does your grammar and vocabulary insure an understanding of the position? You will be judged on your ability to communicate effectively, to speak clearly and concisely, to listen attentively, and respond appropriately to what is said. Your rating will increase if you project self-assurance, and convey your thoughts and answers in a persuasive and convincing fashion. Remember to present good examples of situations to clarify your answers.

- *Interpersonal Skills* – this dimension seeks to measure your skills in human relations, and measure your ability to perceive people problems and propose appropriate solutions or actions. You will also be judged in your ability to interact well with the public, your peers, and management, as demonstrated by judgments about interpersonal situations by your ability to interact well with the interviewer. Do you work harmoniously with others, promote cooperation, and demonstrate sensitivity to the needs of others while maintaining professional relations under adverse conditions? Do you respect ideas from others and praise co-workers or subordinates for outstanding performance? How well do you or could you investigate disputes and complaints? Do you perform or are you involved in any community activities?

- *Motivational Skills* - interviewees who do well in this dimension are those who show that they have taken an active role in improving themselves, and who can motivate others toward self-improvement. Do you show a high degree of motivation, and enthusiasm? Does your employment and education history, in addition to your goals, indicate a steady progression of responsibility? Do you set personal goals that are ambitious, yet attainable?

- *Ability to Assume Responsibility* - this dimension will rate your administrative courage, your inclination to get involved and get the job done. Can you quickly define a problem and gather the pertinent information for solving the problem? Can you logically interpret information, analyze situations, and decide on a course of action? Do you identify alternatives?

Remember to foresee any consequences of the alternatives to your solution.

- **Management Skills** - this dimension will rate your management and supervisory skills, and will concentrate on your ability to apply management theories to job related situations. The following are some of the critical areas in which you will be judged.

    ✓ makes sound decisions promptly
    ✓ uses information to support decisions
    ✓ defends and stands behind decisions
    ✓ delegates effectively and appropriately
    ✓ displays objectivity in stressful situations

ACHIEVEMENTS – projecting your personal and professional achievements is a key to a successful oral interview.

- **Education** – formal education; college degree obtained and graduate studies.
- **Training** – additional on-the-job and technical training; seminars and conferences attended; certifications and special licenses obtained.
- **Honors** – list of honors awarded or received including job related, community, and scholastic honors.
- **Awards** – list of scholastic and professional awards, and certificates.
- **Accomplishments** – miscellaneous professional and personal goals obtained.

YOUR RESPONSES

Interviewers want to get to know the real you. They do not want an idealized portrait of you, but rather a photograph of you as you really are, coupled with your personality traits that may not be as apparent on the outside. So what are we saying, you ask? Don't try to paint a picture of what you think the interviewers want. Be yourself. Let your personality show through. The traits the interviewers are looking for will be summed up by them almost immediately if you present yourself well. Proper preparation will help you accomplish this.

Project a sincere appearance of enthusiasm and confidence. *Listen* to all of the questions. Some interviewers may mumble their questions to test your reaction. Don't panic. Simply ask for the question to be repeated and think before answering. A question may have two or more parts, so listen carefully. Don't shoot from the hip, rather LISTEN, THINK, then FIRE AWAY. You may also be given some rapid-fire questions to determine your reaction. Don't let the pressure show. Control your emotions and remain confident. If you are well prepared, no question is a barrier to achieving your goal.

Keep your answers to the point. Do not ramble. Accentuate the positive and elaborate on the areas in which you have strong expertise. Do not speak in negative terms. Remain loyal to your former supervisors even if you have to bite your lip. Your loyalty will reflect and be viewed as a reflection of your future loyalty. Be professional at all times. Never argue or become negative with the interviewer. Remain in total self-control and emphasize all your unique attributes that positively establish your potential.

Itemize your technical and professional skills that parallel the job requirements. Recall incidents from your experience to illustrate your skills. Meet the job requirements point by point, as the interview unfolds. If your experience is limited, stress your appropriate key personality traits and your desire to learn. Demonstrating that you possess both the skills and positive personality traits to an interviewer will set you apart from the vast majority of job candidates. If you demonstrate that you understand these principles, you will undoubtedly stand out from the rest of the job applicants.

TAKING CONTROL

Make the interviewers believe that you can handle the job without question. You supply the reasons with the way you look, with the enthusiasm, with your personality, with the energy, the confidence, and the ambition you show or don't show. You are in the driver's seat and you control all of these attributes. They are all within you. The interviewers may ask the questions, but if you understand the rules of the game, the scoring process, how you are rated, and have a basic knowledge of what to expect, you can take control of the interviewing process. We all know how to talk, but many of us do not communicate well with groups of people or with people we don't know very well. We speak with our mouths, but we communicate with our eyes, facial expressions, hands, dress, and posture. Communicating is the process of interacting with one another. The object of an oral interview is not just talking or telling the interviewer your ideas, but communicating with the interviewer. You must take control of the interview. We know it is much easier said than done, but the first rule is *not* to take a passive approach in the interviewing process. You must take an active role. The way to do this is to inspire confidence.

SUCCESS FACTORS

The following are the Top Ten reasons job applicants are successful during the interviewing process:

- Showed ambition and motivation
- Had related work experience
- Showed creativity and intelligence
- Conveyed a good personality
- Projected teamwork capabilities
- Fit the job description
- Provided some knowledge of the company
- Showed honesty
- Was well-groomed
- Showed confidence

*Top Ten reasons why people are **not** hired:*
- Lacked proper planning
- Lacked knowledge concerning the position
- Inability to express ones self clearly
- Was not prepared for the interview
- Showed no real interest in the job

- Overbearing
- Overaggressive
- Seemed only interested in the salary of the position
- Poor personal appearance
- Lacked confidence

SIZING UP THE SITUATION

One of the main reasons many candidates fall short in most oral interviews is that they don't inspire confidence. They give the interviewers more reasons to say no than to say yes. In most cases, the reason is a simple matter of fear. It is the fear of failure. We have seen it a dozen times and have fallen victims to it ourselves. Given a choice, many interviewees would rather place their lives in danger than to speak in front of a group of people. Others lose out, not because they don't have the qualifications or can't do the job, but because they fail to properly prepare or lack the enthusiasm and confidence one must display during the oral interview. Quite simply, they didn't sell themselves.

Just like any other problem, one must look at the root cause of the problem. Why do most people lack the ability to perform their best in an oral interview? It is the little nervousness people feel any time there is pressure on them to perform, but a little anxiety is good for you. Understand that you will feel much more nervous than you will look, so don't fall prey to this emotion. The challenge is to control the anxiety and make it work for you, not against you. You control your own destiny, so take control of the situation.

Confidence-
"No one can make you feel inferior without your consent."
Eleanor Roosevelt

Types of Interviews   8

Some say there are two difficult places to be during an oral interview – sitting in front of a desk answering an interviewer's questions and sitting behind the desk asking the questions. Oral interviews differ greatly in make-up and are composed of various types or groups of people. Some interviews are composed of only one interviewer from the department in which the vacancy exists, others are formed by more than one interviewer, while still others are formed by professional personnel directors from the corporate office of a company. No matter what the make-up of the board, the oral interview's importance should not be underestimated.

One must be mentally prepared to be exposed to the various interviewing situations by the different companies you plan to be interviewed by. It is important to keep your responses relevant and to the point. Do not waste precious time telling unrelated war stories or explaining your past hardships. By preparation, confidence, and composing a positive summary of your achievements and management abilities, you will avoid falling prey to mental stress and your emotions. Usually, as we have stated before, there are no specific "right" or "wrong" answers to an interviewer's questions. Rather, it is the various *qualities* of the job candidate's responses dealing with one's professional skills, management abilities, and conceptual knowledge, which are rated.

Several companies have adopted different types of interviews from videoconferencing and telephone interviewing to job fair and on-line computer interviews. Several interview books talk at length about the differences and similarities between these interviews. No matter what innovative or new type of interview a company may come up with through technology, one interview you can bet on that will remain relatively the same is the face-to-face interview with a company official.

QUESTIONING TECHNIQUES

There are, in general terms, two types of oral interviews. You cannot be sure in advance which type of interview you will face, but they are both pretty much the same. In the *general interview*, an interviewer attempts to put you at ease while maintaining a professional standard of scoring your responses to the questions asked. The interviewer will permit you to demonstrate those intangible qualities for which he or she is searching. Within the general interview there are three types of questioning procedures. Although the questioning techniques are mildly different, your responses should remain relatively the same.

Direct Interview – the direct interview walks you through the interviewing process as the interviewer asks you questions directly from a prepared question list and records your responses.

Non-Direct Interview – the non-direct interview asks the interviewee very general and broad questions. This interviewer or questioning technique rewards you for leading the discussion. This type of interview allows you to elaborate on your achievements, so by all means toot your own horn.

Behavior-Based Interview – the type of questioning of the behavior-based interview relies on your ability for storytelling. The interviewee answers questions and relays experiences to back up their responses. This is the most frequently used interviewing technique. Many experts and employers alike, believe your past behavior will predict your future behavior as an employee.

The second type of interview is the *stress interview*. In this type of interview, there is no attempt to put you at ease, but rather to put pressure on you. This is often accomplished by firing questions at you in a machine gun fashion, seldom letting you finish an answer

TYPES OF INTERVIEWS 8-3

to one question before being faced with another. A more subtle approach is giving you the impression the interviewer is not paying attention to you when you are speaking by looking around the room or looking out the window. Other examples include long pauses between questions to challenging your responses. Don't let this type of interview make you become unglued. The interviewers are seeking to determine your ability to maintain a calm composure while in a stressful situation. They are also seeking to determine if you will break down or become distracted in pressure type situations, and how your judgment may be affected by stress.

Generally speaking, most companies have gotten away from the stress type interview, but if you do encounter one do not let it upset you. Don't give the interviewers any ammunition or indication that their actions bother you. Remain calm and controlled. No one will be able to put more pressure on you than yourself. Your preparedness will help keep you composed.

Remember, you can control the interview. If an interviewer *seems* not to be paying attention to your responses, don't be fooled. They are hanging on your every word. Attempt to gain eye contact with the interviewer to bring him or her back aligned with you. During rapid fired questions, take a moment before you respond to slow the pace. Don't get caught in their trap by answering the questions too quickly. Your questions will surely be shallow and incomplete at best. Some interviewers may try to play tricks on you, but understand they are only trying to sort out the best possible job candidates. Remember, no one can intimidate you without your permission.

INAPPROPRIATE QUESTIONS

In the forthcoming chapters we will prepare you with a number of potential oral interview questions that are appropriate during the hiring process. However, there are some questions that are considered inappropriate. Several cases brought before the attention of the Equal Employment Opportunity Commission (EEOC) and the appellate courts, have caused a number of questions to be restricted by employers. The questions that follow are prohibited from being asked during an oral interview or as part of an application for employment.

✗ Questions involving sex - unless the position specifically requires a particular sex, the employer cannot make comments or notes regarding the candidate's sex.

✗ Questions involving religion – it is unlawful for an employer to ask questions regarding religious faith.

✗ Questions involving national origin – it is unlawful for an employer to ask questions regarding national origin.

✗ Questions involving marital status – an employer may not ask the candidate if he or she is married, single, divorced or engaged. This information can be discovered *after* employment has been obtained or for insurance purposes.

✗ Questions involving children – a potential employer may not ask a candidate if he or she has children, their ages, how many, or questions involving child-care. This information can be discovered *after* employment for insurance purposes.

✗ Questions involving personal physical information – a potential employer may not ask a candidate as to his or her weight, height, etc.

✗ Questions involving military record – a potential employer may not ask a candidate as to the type of discharge he or she received from the military, or what branch of the military the candidate served in.

✗ Questions regarding age - a potential employer may not ask a candidate as to his/her age, or approximate age. It is permissible to determine if the candidate is over the age of eighteen for employment that requires an adult by law.

✗ Questions regarding housing – a potential employer may not ask the candidate if he or she owns or rents a home, or the type of home. An employer may ask for a candidate's

TYPES OF INTERVIEWS   8-5

address, but it is generally unlawful to press for more information beyond this point.

✗ Questions involving a criminal record – a potential employer may not ask a candidate if he or she has ever been arrested. However, an employer may ask a candidate if he or she has ever been convicted of a crime and where and when it took place. Background checks are permissible in obtaining criminal arrest history for security clearance purposes.

Below are just a few sample questions that are inappropriate to ask a candidate. If such a question is asked during an oral interview, (this is a judgement call on your part) the candidate should politely indicate so to the person during the interview and inform the interviewer that you choose not to answer the question. If employment is denied, the candidate should contact the EEOC and inform the agency of the circumstances.

- What does your spouse do for a living?
- What is your first language?
- Have you ever been in the militia of a foreign country?
- When and why were you discharged from the military?
- How many of your relatives live with you?
- Do you need to arrange time for child care?
- Are you disabled?
- Where were you born?
- Are you a member of the local country club?
- Are you currently married?
- Do you plan to start a family?
- Do you have a girlfriend?
- Do you have a boyfriend?
- What is your sexual preference?
- What branch of the military did you serve in?
- How old are you?
- Are you in good health?
- When were you born?
- Do you regularly attend a church, temple, or mosque?
- Have you encountered any health problems recently?

- Have you ever been arrested?
- What is your religion?
- How do you feel about gay marriages?
- Do you have a family?
- How many children do you have?
- What is your net worth?
- Does your wife/husband stay at home to care for the children?
- Do you devote any time or financial resources to charity work?

COMMUNICATION SKILLS

Communication skills are among the most desired qualities employers say they want most out of their employees. Why are communications skills so vitally important? It is the only way an employer can truly get to know their employees. Your voice has one basic function. The basic function is to communicate, so make sure that you speak clearly. Whispering, mumbling, or speaking too loudly creates a bad impression.

When interviewing, speak like a professional. Punctuating your speech with pauses will make you appear thoughtful. If you want to indicate conviction and decisiveness, drop the pitch of your voice at the end of a statement. Speak conservatively, but at the same time pronounce all the sounds, letters, and syllables in the words you use. Using proper grammar positions you as an educated and intelligent person. Never weaken your responses with filler phrases such as, "like," "Okay," "you know," or "uhm hum." You may find your interview cut short by such nervous or bad habits.

Remember what personal and professional traits employers are looking for in a job applicant. Given a choice of technically equal applicants, employers almost always choose the job applicant they like the best. Despite the best efforts of using the various interviewing techniques, most experts agree that more people lose job offers for personality factors than for lack of capability. Listed

TYPES OF INTERVIEWS   8-7

below is a list of personality factors employers are searching for in job applicants:

- ☺ Assertiveness
- ☺ Dependability
- ☺ Optimistic
- ☺ Sociable
- ☺ Conscientious
- ☺ Tolerance
- ☺ Responsibility
- ☺ Trustworthiness
- ☺ Imagination
- ☺ Emotionally Stable
- ☺ Intellectually Curious
- ☺ Open to New Experiences
- ☺ Positive Resilience – able to bounce back from failure
- ☺ Self-Control – personal control over one's destiny
- ☺ Empathy – the ability to sympathize with another's feelings
- ☺ Achievement Oriented – drive to obtain goals

Here are several other *key points* that may assist you in your studying and preparation for the oral interview.

🔑 Keep a copy of your application or resume and review it carefully before the interview. The interviewer most likely has already received these documents, and they may be used as a starting point for the interview. Know what you have listed as experience, training, education, and the sequence of the dates. An Interviewer may ask you to recite the information contained in the document.

🔑 Study the specifications and qualifications set forth in the job announcement. The interviewer may have the specifications of the position in front of him or her to use as a guide. The qualities, characteristics, and knowledge required for the position will be stated in the document. It also adds valuable information as to the nature of the oral interviewing process. An applicant for a position or promotion must thoroughly know the duties and responsibilities of the job he or she is seeking. You must prepare yourself to solve hypothetical problems, and answer questions which will reveal your understanding of the job. Never go into an oral interview without understanding the duties and responsibilities of the position you hope to fill.

- Go over the company's annual report or other related information you have researched. The more you prepare, the more confident you will become.

- Arrive at least fifteen minutes early and bring with you business-related (i.e. *Fortune, Business Week, Money,* or *Forbes*) magazines to read while waiting. What is not impressive is an applicant just twiddling their thumbs waiting for their name to be called or reading last week's edition of a supermarket tabloid.

- Treat the receptionist or secretary with the utmost respect. The secretary can be your best friend or your worst enemy in trying to obtain a job. Many interviewers will ask the secretary or receptionist their opinion of an applicant.

- Go into the interview with the assumption the worst interviewer in the world will interview you. This will increase your confidence and you will be able to steer the interview the way you want it to go. Act like a consultant and not an interviewee. Remember, you can control the interview with the way you present yourself and the information you want to convey.

- If possible, prior to your scheduled interview, talk with some of the employees or supervisors who currently hold the position you seek. Find out what they expect and hope for in the way of job performance. Think about your background, and your own personal experiences and qualities in terms of work and management abilities. Prepare yourself to relate those qualities to the interviewer.

- 🔑 Relax and stay calm. The interviewer is often just as concerned with impressing you as you are with impressing him or her.

- 🔑 Think through each qualification required. How would you go about questioning someone to assure yourself that he or she is qualified? How would you answer those questions? Try to visualize the kind of questions you would ask if you were the interviewer. How well could you answer them? Be frank and realistic with yourself. Find your weaknesses and work on them. Patch up the holes in your armor before you walk into the interview room to do battle.

- 🔑 Display a mature sense of humor. In most cases, a healthy sense of humor is a big plus, but don't over do it. Remember, employers are searching for competent people they will feel comfortable and enjoy working with.

- 🔑 Do some general reading in areas in which you feel you may be weak. The advantage of general reading is that it helps you consolidate and organize the thinking process.

- 🔑 Watch your health, and most importantly your mental attitude. Get plenty of sleep and watch your diet. You want to be in the best possible mental and physical condition during your studying and interviewing phase.

RULES OF THE GAME

The oral interview is one of the most subjective aspects of the hiring process. The problem is that the oral interview is very much a game, but the rules seldom change while the interviewer is playing out his or her role. Pay attention not only to what you say, but *how* you are responding. The interviewer is making an evaluation of everything you say and do by judging your ability, experience, and personality to determine whether you are qualified for the job. Your fate is determined not so much by your qualifications, but how you rate in your interview performance in general. Basically, how you play the game. Knowing the rules of the game as explained in the previous chapters will help you and your overall success. Your task in the game is to make a sale. You are the salesman, and the product you are selling is yourself. The asset of the product is your ability to communicate to inform interviewer that you are the best person for the job. If you just answer an interviewer's questions, you will not distinguish yourself from the seemingly countless others that the interviewer will encounter. Instead, unleash the timely preparation you have put forth, and you will be well on your way as a professional in your chosen profession.

Confidence-
"They do all, because they think they can."
Virgil (100 - 19 BC) Roman Poet

Dressing Sharp 9

Most company interviews do not *formally* evaluate a candidate's appearance, however, your appearance is the interviewer's first impression of you. We judge people, sometimes unfairly, by our first impressions. The moment we set eyes on someone, our minds start to make judgments and evaluations. All companies require a certain minimal level of professionalism in the way their employees dress. Interviewees must be expected to exceed these standards. Companies are made up of people working together as a group. If your clothing or grooming sends a message that you are different from the group, you may send an immediate negative image of yourself. This is why choosing your clothing is so important. Visual assessments reveal aspects of character and personality that are determined by the perceptions of the interviewer.

FIRST IMPRESSIONS

As assessors we can tell you from experience that from the second an interviewee walks through the doorway, he or she is inspected from top to bottom, thus a first impression is created. It can set the tone of the interview and the process continues through the entire questioning phase, especially if the rater is impressed or extremely unimpressed with the way you present yourself. For some interviewers it may sway him or her in determining whether or not to hire you. Many interviewers make a subconscious decision within seconds of meeting an interviewee and spend the rest of the time during the interview validating their first impression. Because of the competitive nature of the entire interviewing process, it is important to secure any and every possible advantage you can. The correct image you display during the oral interview process will give you an edge over your competition.

So, what does this all mean? It means look crisp and dress sharp. Polish the brass and gold trim on all of your armor. Project a professional image. Look the part. When you look good, you feel good and when you feel good, your confidence level increases. Likewise, if a job candidate cannot put himself together in a professional manner, why should an interviewer assume the interviewee can put it together on the job? The message that you radiate is in direct proportion to the visual image that you project before you have a chance to say a word. Our appearance tells others how we feel about ourselves. Your overall appearance will leave the most tangible impression, and your presentation will be influenced in the mind of the interviewers by the way you look and by the way you present yourself. It is the little things you do or don't do that determine a prospective employer's first impression of you.

Consider this for a moment. What are your perceptions of someone who wears an inexpensive, brown vinyl jacket with shirt and tie adorned with flashy gold-nugget jewelry as opposed to someone wearing a tailored-made wool-blend navy blue pinstriped suit? How about a woman dressed in a short skin-tight skirt and low plunging neckline blouse? Do you immediately conjure up impressions of these imaginary people? Of course you do, it's human nature. The same thing happens to the people interviewing you. Their subconscious biases size you up the minute they meet you.

When you choose to wear business attire, our advice, along with many others, is to dress conservatively and be well groomed. Do it right. Go to a leading department store and buy a new suit, new shirt, new belt, new tie, new socks, and new shoes. After all, it is a good excuse to buy some new clothes, and you can get some use out of them after the interview. Taking the time to present an attractive, professional image before the interview will add to your confidence.

As you develop and expand your wardrobe, avoid transient fads. Do you remember Nehru jackets, leisure-suits, and wide ties? Sure you do. The reason why we mention this is because on any given day we can point out people who actually believe these styles are still fashionable. What we mean is, leave the 1970's era white polyester suit and black shirt hanging in your closet, but don't worry, they say Disco will eventually come back in style.

Whether your new to the job field or not, you can adapt your image to play up to your strengths and minimize stereotypes. When you set your sights on a potential employer, pay close attention to what the management staff is wearing, and then dress better. Keep your style attractive and up-to-date, but be careful that you don't give the impression of being too faddish. Go classic and conservative. Use every advantage within your control to get hired or promoted.

BUSINESS DRESS FOR MEN

Despite the current fashion trends, location, and season certain conservative and traditional suits appear to be always in style. This makes life pretty easy for men, since business suit fashions tend not to change dramatically from year to year. The power look for men is a conservative business type suit. Stick to the basics. To maximize your image, choose an authoritative, professional look. Don't fall prey to the casual business look of khaki pants and a sport jacket. This look will probably be okay once you get the job, but wait until after you are hired. Likewise, three-piece suits are outdated and may seem pretentious. Use good judgment when making this decision. For the interview men should choose traditional dark suits in the various shades of navy blue or gray, either pin-striped or solid. Natural wool fabrics generally drape the body better than synthetics, so stay away from the inexpensive polyester suits and ensure that the clothes you select fit comfortably and properly. Clothes will not look good on you if they do not fit properly, regardless of how expensive they are.

SHIRTS

Basic light colored shirts are the best, with solid-white still the traditional favorite. When interviewing, never wear a dark colored shirt. The paler and more subtle the shade, the better the impression you will make. The shirt cuffs should be showing about one inch below your coat sleeve, adding a touch of class and style. Cotton shirts look better than their synthetic counterparts. A cotton and polyester blended shirt can be an acceptable alternative, but keep in mind the higher the cotton content, the better the shirt will look. Have your new shirt dry cleaned with heavy starch and be sure to try on your clothes long before the actual interview. You don't want to find out one hour before the interview that you are missing a shirt button or the zipper on your trousers won't close properly. This may seem like trivial advice now, but it will be a major event if it happens shortly before the interview.

TIES

Bow ties are not appropriate for a job interview. While a cheap looking tie can ruin an expensive suit, the right tie can do wonders for a not-so-perfect suit in displaying a professional image. A pure silk tie or silk and wool blend is the best bet for your interview. Ties should be conservatively worn in one of the following patterns: paisleys, stripes, or prints. Stay away from plaids or solids. The colors should accent the suit, not match it. Red ties command attention and are associated with power, but be careful not to over do it. Learn the proper way to knot a tie. Nothing takes away from a sharp looking suit faster than a poorly tied knot. Lastly, the length of the tie should extend to your belt.

SOCKS

As with the tie, socks should complement the suit, but unlike the tie they should match the color of your pants to avoid attracting unfavorable attention. Your socks should be worn with the length long enough so that they cover your calf when your are sitting. The most favorable socks are the elastic, over-the-calf type socks.

SHOES
Shoes should be black, brown, or cordovan and made of leather. Wingtips have been a popular choice for decades and are universally accepted. Almost equally conservative are basic slip-on shoes with a low heel and tassel.

ACCESSORIES
The wrong accessories can destroy the professional image of any candidate. Basic rings and watches are acceptable as long as they are modest in taste. If you choose to wear a ring or watch, it should be conservative, plain and simple. Do not wear any religious or political pins.

For men, earrings, noserings, eyebrowrings, or whatever the latest fashion trend may be at the present time, should not be worn during an interview regardless of your personal tastes. It usually will not fit the management or conservative company look.

Belts should be worn to match or complement your shoes. Stick to plain leather belts of good quality. In regard to belt buckles, they too should be plain and conservative. The interview is not the place to show off your newly purchased, over-sized, chrome-plated, rodeo rider belt buckle.

BUSINESS DRESS FOR WOMEN

Choosing a conservative look for women is a little more complicated. Women have more choices in dress and, therefore, can make more mistakes. Can women dress too intimidating? Some people think so, especially younger male bosses. The best bet for women is to choose conservative suits and dresses, and avoid extremes in length, color, and frills. Stay away from pants, miniskirts, sweaters, and anything that is overly trendy or casual. Women should choose a contemporary-styled two piece business suit or dress. For the interview, avoid the color red and other bold colors, rather choose seasonal colors, with navy blue being a year-round favorite. Fabric selection depends on the season and the outfit. Cotton and polyester blends are a good choice and they lessen the wrinkability factor of the garment. Whether you select a skirt or suit is your choice.

BLOUSES
Blouses should be conservative in style. Light pastel blouses or complementing tops are always in good taste. Long sleeves project a professional image, so stay away from sleeveless blouses.

ACCESSORIES
Contrasting belts or scarves can add color to an outfit. Just as cheap looking ties can take away from an expensive suit for men, so can a cheap looking scarf for women, so be careful with your selection if you choose to wear a scarf. Fashionable basic pumps are always in vogue as long as they have a conservative heel height. Women have a greater range in color selection than men do regarding shoes. The shoes should be leather and complement the outfit. With regard to belts, it is the same as with the men. Belts should match or complement the shoes. If the belt is overly noticeable it may be wrong for the outfit.

Jewelry and accessories should be modestly worn. You can personalize your clothing with tasteful understated jewelry and accessories, just remember not to over do it. The saying, "less is more" cannot be overstated when it comes to jewelry. One necklace and a bracelet are acceptable, but anything around the ankle should be left at home during the interview process.

Hosiery should be non-textured and in shades of neutral depending on the outfit. Hosiery should not make a statement of their own. Hosiery and pantyhose are prone to run at the worst of times, so be sure to carry an extra pair with you on the day of the oral interview. A general rule is that at least two out of three of your accessories (shoes, skirt, hose) should be of the same color.

Women may want to carry a briefcase to an interview. A briefcase is a symbol of authority and an excellent choice. Do not, however, bring both a purse and a briefcase with you to an interview. It will be cumbersome for you trying to manage both. Place your essentials in a small pouch inside the briefcase if you choose to carry one.

Lastly, but very importantly, do not use heavy or excessive makeup. You want to give a natural, businesslike impression. Eye make-up, especially, should be subtle. Apply your lipstick, face and eye makeup sparingly being careful to use natural, subdued tones. Remember, you want to fit the look of a business professional.

MISCELLEANOUS TIPS

Your mind will probably be racing as you anticipate what you will say and how you will act, but the first impression you create will be visual, and the importance of body language, grooming, and dress should not be underestimated. Remember to polish your shoes. Unshined, unpolished shoes or those with worn heels make a poor impression. Shoes are one of the first things, and last things, an interviewer notices as you pass through the doorway.

Hairstyles portray certain images. Ensure that your hair is neat. Decide beforehand if you need hair spray, it may be windy on the day of your oral interview. Think about whether you may need an umbrella or raincoat. The point of all of this is to prepare beforehand, *not* the day of your interview. You will be too preoccupied with the material you have studied and researched along with a dozen other things.

If you smoke, *don't* before an interview. We know, even non-smokers will feel like they may want to smoke a carton before their name is called, but some people get very offended by the odor of cigarette smoke and you surely don't want to offend your interviewer. If you must smoke, be sure to freshen your breath with chewing gum or mints *before* you go into the interview room, not while you are in the interview room. Never chew gum during an interview. Gum will actually take away from your mouth's natural tendency to salivate, *once it is removed*. Be conscious of the fact that cigarette smoke will also cling to your clothing. Non-smokers can pick up on this immediately. If you use cologne, don't over do it. Again, this can send a negative message, much like cigarette odor.

This should go without saying, but don't overlook the obvious of being well groomed. Cleanliness with properly trimmed and cleaned fingernails is a must. Make sure your nails are clean and neatly trimmed. So don't plan on overhauling your car engine the day before the interview. Dirty fingernails can result in a negative feeling from an interviewer you may not be able to overcome, unless of course you are being interviewed for the position of diesel mechanic.

Women with painted nails should stick to clear or a lightly colored polish; no blues, greens, neons, or overly decorative nails. Much of these tips are common sense, but they are often overlooked or not thought about until the day of the interview.

YOUR MANNER AND BEHAVIOR

Another part of appearance that employers consider when interviewing potential employees is their manner. Manner refers to your personal behavior. How you behave in an interview gives the employer an idea of how you will behave on the job. Since you have very little time to make an impression, your manner will greatly affect the impression you project to an interviewer. Your manner during an interview should be natural and positive. Your manner will demonstrate good appearance if you conduct yourself with confidence. Needless to say, you should always show employers common courtesy. Honesty and sincerity are elements of a positive manner.

CHECKLIST

The following contains a quick checklist of "dressing sharp" for men and women during the oral interviewing process:

For *men*, the checklist includes the following:
- ✓ Dress in a conservative suit
- ✓ Ensure your tie complements the suit
- ✓ No bulges in the pockets
- ✓ No battered briefcases
- ✓ Wear over-the-calf socks
- ✓ Have a fresh shave and trimmed, clean hair

For *women*, the checklist includes:
- ✓ Choose a conservative look
- ✓ No short hemlines
- ✓ No plunging necklines
- ✓ No see-through fabrics
- ✓ No tight-fitting clothing
- ✓ No heavy make-up
- ✓ No chipped nails
- ✓ No hosiery runs

For *everyone*, the checklist includes:
- ✓ Be well-groomed
- ✓ Polish your shoes
- ✓ Censor your breath
- ✓ Avoid heavy fragrances
- ✓ Ensure your fingernails are clean
- ✓ No sunglasses
- ✓ No fad watches or flashy jewelry
- ✓ Do not wear any religious or political pins

Keeping up with fashion trends by reading the various men and women's fashion magazines is good advice, but don't go overboard with their trendy advice. To sum it up, dress to fit the role. Before the interview, observe what the people already employed are wearing. The initial appearance you make will create a presumption that will have a strong effect on the rest of the interview. You can prove your qualifications before saying a word, so use every advantage you can. Dress like you would like to be perceived. When choosing your dress for your oral interview, remember the expression - *clothes make the person.*

Appearance-
"It's only shallow people who do *not* judge by appearance."
Oscar Wilde (1854 -1900) Irish Poet

The Big Day   **10**

THE ORAL INTERVIEW DAY

The oral interview day has finally arrived. It is important to be well groomed, scrubbed, trimmed, and as immaculately fresh as possible. Plan to arrive early, allowing plenty of time to get to the oral interview location so you can account for the unexpected, such as car problems or unusually heavy traffic delays. You do not want to feel rushed. Arriving early will also help you to relax and give you time to gather your thoughts. Unfortunately, the butterflies in all likelihood will still be there. Do not worry, it is a normal physiological response. The time you have before the interview should be used to collect your thoughts and reflect upon your preparation.

Prepare yourself mentally. This is the time to pump yourself up and boost your confidence. Remember, most fights are won or lost before the first punch is thrown. Realize this is your time. Look forward to the questions an interviewer will ask you. You have prepared long and hard for this day. There is not a question anyone could possibly ask that you will not have a response to. Relax your mind and body. Let your confidence and poise show through. Believe us, this is half the battle. Interviewers like seeing a relaxed candidate.

Freshen up in the wash room before the interview. Check yourself over from head to toe. You don't want to be traipsing into the oral interview room with a sheet of toilet paper stuck on the bottom of your shoe. A close friend of ours relayed to us that during one of his promotional interviews, he found out that his shirttail was sticking out through the unzipped fly of his pants. Unfortunately, he discovered this *after* leaving the interview room. It was one of life's most embarrassing moments. Another friend told us how he gave a great interview and when it was time to leave the room he uncrossed his legs and stood up, only to find that one of his legs had completely fallen asleep. He then proceeded to drag his seemingly lifeless limb from the interview room. Not a very good exit or last impression.

You want to look your business best, and your first impression as well as your last impression is vitally important. Just like most people judge a book by its cover, so do interviewers. Your first impression made upon the interviewers cannot be overstated. Within the first couple of minutes the assessors have already summed you up. The first minutes during the oral interview are critical. Here are some quick reminders:

- Walk tall and slowly, but deliberately, into the interview room. Be Genuine. Smile, not with just the mouth, but with your eyes as well. Present a relaxed, not cocky, appearance.

- Maintain direct eye contact throughout the interview, but don't stare. Maintaining eye contact projects confidence and self-assurance. If you become nervous and have an indication to look down or away, catch yourself and look back at your interviewers.

- Respond with words when greeting your interviewers with something to the effect, "It's nice to meet you," "It's a pleasure meeting you," or something along these lines.

- A firm, but gentle handshake accompanied with a genuine smile and direct eye contact sets a positive tone and makes a tremendous impression on an interviewer. The interviewers get a nonverbal message that this is a straightforward, confident person. Be mindful of your handshake. It should be firm, not bone crushing. You are not in an arm wrestling match with the interviewers. You also don't want a clammy, floppy-fish handshake. Make sure your hands are dry before entering the interview room, even if it means wiping your hands inconspicuously on your clothing *before* entering the interview room. Keeping a handkerchief in your pocket adds some security for damp, clammy hands. It also provides extra security for that unforeseen sneeze in the interview room that could cause you some problems.

Remember to convey a genuine and confident appearance. It is only natural to feel a little uneasy going into the room, but by now you should have overcome the fear of the oral interview. You have prepared yourself. This is your interview. Take control and walk tall. Do not take a subordinate role. Remember the position you are applying for. If you put your best foot forward, the rest will follow. Package a positive image. Exude enthusiasm and energy. Project dependability, loyalty, honesty, efficiency, and pride in your accomplishments and abilities.

ALIGN YOURSELF WITH THE INTERVIEWERS

Create a bond with the interviewers. Will Rogers once said, "I never met a man I didn't like." Be pleasant and align yourself with the interviewers. Have you ever wondered why some people seem to get everything they always go after? It is no secret. It is the self-assurance and confidence they have in themselves. Thus, they project confidence. They are liked by others who want to align themselves with them. They simply learn that liking others has a positive effect. It evokes a powerful rule of human emotion. People like people who like themselves. You will never get anything from anyone if they feel they are not liked or respected by you.

Another psychological rule of human emotion is that we like people who are like ourselves. Now think about that for a moment. Think about your close friends, your spouse, who you voted for in past political elections, and even some sports figures you admire. If a sports figure or celebrity you simply did not like for whatever reason was endorsing a product, you will tend *not* to purchase the product. If you can make an interviewer see him or herself in you, you will have won him over. One of the ways to do this is to talk to (not at) each interviewer. This is especially true when there is someone on the panel who seemingly is not paying attention to you, or worse yet is trying to distract you. If an interviewer fits this criteria, make sure you give him or her special attention. Smile at the interviewer. Talk directly to the interviewer. Show the interviewers they are not getting to you, rather you are responding to a stressful situation with control.

In Chapter Three we talked about gathering information if at all possible about those who will be interviewing you. This is the time to use the information to align yourself with one, if not all of the interviewers. This is a great time to point out things you enjoy or specialize in which you know one (or more) of the interviewers has an interest in. Topics that you may have in common could include:

- 👍 Sports or Hobbies
- 👍 Hometown
- 👍 College or University
- 👍 Major or Degree
- 👍 Job Position
- 👍 Management Style
- 👍 Professional Articles Written
- 👍 Shared Work Ethics
- 👍 Career Track
- 👍 Specialized Training

If you think about it, we sum up people every day. "His hair is too long," or "she wearing too much make-up," are statements we have probably heard before. We assess people and approve or disapprove of them based on an initial observation. We then tend to look for things to reinforce our judgment. Is this stereotyping?

Yes it is. Is it unfair? Is it prejudicial? Yes it is, but it is human nature.

THE ORAL INTERVIEW

When you are called to the room (the one you are already familiar with), take a few cleansing breaths and button your suit jacket or smooth out your skirt before walking through the doorway. Walk in proudly with command presence. Don't be in a hurry to sit down, you are not being timed. Acknowledge the interviewers and firmly, but gently, shake each interviewer's hand. Try to remember each interviewers' name or at least their title or rank and wait until you are offered a seat before you sit down.

You should appear calm and comfortable, whatever your internal thoughts may be. Sit in a natural position, bearing in mind that you are not on your couch at home. Avoid crossing your arms across your chest, crossing your legs, or looking too laid back. This is often perceived as an indication that you want to close people out. You do not want to send a disrespectful message. When you sit down, make sure to unbutton your suit jacket, position the chair comfortably up to the desk or table, and sit up straight. As you are seated, it is usually the time when you will be given instructions such as the length of the interview, the number of questions you will be expected to answer, or other pertinent information. Listen carefully and collect your thoughts.

Often your interview will begin with an introductory remark, such as, "Is there anything you would like to say before we begin," or "Tell us a little something about yourself." Some interviews are even more direct and specific - "You'll have a maximum of four minutes to give your Opening Statement. I will let you know when your time is up. You may continue with your Opening if you have not finished within the allotted time, however, keep in mind this will take away from your time to answer the questions which may effect your overall score." No matter what the case may be, pause momentarily, gather your thoughts, then dive in with enthusiasm. As you are delivering your Opening Statement, use this time to relax and show your preparation. Check yourself. Are you sitting up straight in the chair? Are you projecting self-confidence?

Make sure you maintain eye contact and align yourself with the interviewers. Do not worry if you have missed a point or two, and don't worry about hitting each word you have practiced. If you draw a blank, realize where you left off and continue talking about your career, education, and accomplishments. After the delivery of your Opening Statement, you will feel much more relaxed. You may even have a drop of saliva left in your dry mouth at this point.

The next segment of the interview will be the set of questions to test your abilities to fill the position. All of your preparation will now pay off. As the questions are being asked, listen carefully. You must comprehend if there is more than one part to a question. You don't want to be caught short by answering only part of a question. In some very formal oral interviews, the assessors are not permitted to explain a question. Normally, you may only ask for the question to be repeated. Fortunately, this is not this case in most business interviews. Before answering a question, pause briefly and gather your thoughts. Do not rush to answer each question too quickly by shooting from the hip to show off your quick grasp of the subject matter. It will only show your immaturity. The assessors will be more attentive to your rudeness than with your quickness to respond.

When answering a question, get right to the point as soon as possible. Do not hide the fact that you know the answer by adding extraneous comments first. Articulate your answers clearly and concisely. Once you have answered a question directly, expound upon your response. Support your response with examples, studies, theories, and factual data. Take time to reveal your philosophy and depth on the subject. Look at the Big Picture. Tell the interviewers why it is important to take the actions you did. If it is an employee problem, remember your interpersonal skills. Not only do you want to correct a problem, but you want to find out what may be the underlying cause so that you can prevent any future mishaps from occurring. Use the Power Words you have studied and incorporate the words in your responses. Show your resourcefulness and your ability to be innovative to solve a problem. The bottom line is that you can be creative as possible in order to create the best answer to a question.

When you are finished with your response to a question, let the assessors know you are finished. Do not let your voice trail off to a mumble at the end of a response. Reflect on the chapter that explained and covered closing a response, then close with authority. There is nothing more aggravating than to hear something like (with a shrug of the shoulders), "that's about it." Yeah, you've got that right. That *is* about it. You have just destroyed a perfectly good response with this type of conclusion. You must end your response with some type of closing, such as, "to bring it all together," "to sum up what I have just said in a few words," or "in closing I would like to emphasize." Then *briefly* state in a sentence or two the main points of your delivery. Do not rehash everything and don't babble or belabor the points. When you are finished, stop.

By pushing points in some detail, an interviewer learns something about your understanding of principles, your ability to think and express yourself clearly, your judgment, your convictions, and a little something about your temperament, attitude, and knowledge. However irritating some questions may be, state your answers sincerely and purposeful. You must project enthusiasm and display an interest in the interview. Here are some helpful tips to remember during the interview phase:

- **Get Comfortable.** Sit comfortably, erect, and relaxed, rather than stiff and rigid. Be mindful of your hands. Your hands may be occasionally useful to emphasize a point, but do not let them detract from your presentation by becoming a point of distraction. Don't fumble with trinkets or personal items. Sit with your hands folded on the table in front of you. This allows for easy use of your hands, and displays a somewhat aggressive and confident posture. It also keeps you from hitting your hands on the table as you bring them up to stress a point.

- **Be Courteous.** Do not chew gum or look at your watch, as this can be construed as disrespectful or impolite. Do the small things that help people feel at ease. Your behavior throughout the interview should show that you know how to get along with people and that you can maintain a pleasant relationship, regardless of the circumstances.

- **Be Yourself.** Keep your attitude confident. Be pleasant, but not chummy. Smile, but avoid artificial grinning or pleasantness. Watch your grammar and avoid slang expressions. Speaking well does not require exaggerated or stilted language. We speak to people everyday without bumbling through each word, let this day be the same.

- **Be Attentive.** Time is limited, so don't waste it. Do not give all of your attention to just one member of the interview board. If you have more than one assessor interviewing you, each assessor will usually have an equal weight in evaluating you. Different members may use various approaches in questioning, so be alert for a change in tactics or a change in subject matter. If an interviewer is starting a lengthy problem for you to analyze, do not interrupt or "jump the gun" by giving a response too quickly. Let the assessor fully state the question before replying or asking for the question to be repeated. Be sure to *listen* carefully to avoid having every question repeated. Having *every* question repeated will not sit well with the panel members.

- **Be Truthful.** Experienced interviewers are skillful in recognizing contradictions or weaknesses in exaggerated descriptions of personal qualifications. An interviewer who suspects a "snow job" will develop serious doubts about a candidate's abilities, and the candidate may soon find himself being shuffled out the door.

- **Think Before Answering.** Reply promptly, but not hastily. Pause momentarily before answering. Inappropriate or unorganized replies usually come from talking before you have considered your reply carefully.

- **Be Resolute.** Defend your position in matters of opinion with facts or illustrated experiences. Interviewers are more interested in seeing how you can justify your response than they are in having you agree with them. Do not start a debate, yet do not surrender a good position. If your position is worth taking, then it is worth defending. However, if you see an error in your logic have the courage to recognize your mistake. This will only cause the assessors to rate you highly in areas of flexibility and good judgment.

- **Keep the Purpose of the Interview in Mind.** Avoid trying to match wits with the interviewer. Do not try to give answers that you think they want. Give an honest assessment of the situation or problem, then state your answer. Be objective in your responses. If you feel a member of the panel is being critical, by all means do not become antagonistic. Do not get caught falling into their trap. The assessor who becomes critical is probably doing it for a reason, most likely to test your abilities in a stressful situation.

- **Be Brief and Use Understandable Words.** Do not be overly technical. Many good responses have been weakened by the injection of slang terms or technical jargon. Recall what we said earlier, and do not try to sound smarter or older than you are. Instead, BE YOURSELF. You will find that your responses will flow much easier. Do not use words that you normally do not use, or have a hard time pronouncing. This will ensure that your concentration will remain focused on the topic at hand and not on your last mutilation of the English language. Also, be mindful of your grammar and do not dominate your responses by trying to show all you know about a subject. Answer the questions directly, then expound upon your responses.

- **Leave with a Strong Closing.** Develop a memorable and powerful closing. This is normally the last thing the interviewers will hear before the scoring begins. The way you leave the interview will also leave an impression with the interviewers. Conclude the interview by summarizing your skills and telling how they will benefit the company. Very briefly, in less than a minute, highlight your abilities to handle people, information, and things. Always depart in the same polite and assured manner as you entered the interview room. Smile, use direct eye contact, and offer to shake the interviewers' hands. Lastly, but very importantly, express your appreciation for the interviewers' time.

Enthusiasm-
"Nothing great was ever achieved without enthusiasm."
Ralph Waldo Emerson (1803-1882) American Philosopher

Interview Questions 11

Every employer wants to know whether or not you will fit in with the company, what you can contribute to the company, and whether you are manageable. The following five hundred sample oral interview questions or similar variations are commonly used for evaluation purposes by various companies. The questions are geared toward gaining insight into your past behavior and attitude. It is universally believed that your past actions predict future behavior. You must be able to articulate key aspects of yourself in the interview to look and act the part of a self-confident and successful person. One of the best ways to prepare for an interview is to script your answers to key interview questions. In preparing your answers to the questions, think of yourself as a candidate in a political campaign. A skillful candidate is focused on the message he or she wants to convey, rather than being led by an interviewer's questions. Stay in control with your responses. Articulate what you want the interviewer to remember. Be prepared to convince an interviewer that you are uniquely qualified to make a contribution to the company.

Try to visualize the kind of questions you would ask if you were an interviewer. How well can you answer an interviewer's questions? Try to appraise your knowledge and background in each area against the position you seek, and identify your weak areas. Take the time to answer the questions and write out your responses. It is a lot of work, but it will help prepare you in going through the various problem-solving steps when faced with a particular challenge and incorporating a closing to each answer. Answer the questions honestly, rather than the way you think an interviewer may want you to answer them. Interviewers will generally spot this practice and if they think you are less than honest you can forget about the job. Be critical of your responses as you review the questions, but be realistic. Remember you are your own worst critic, so don't be too hard on yourself.

PERSONAL PROFILE QUESTIONS
1. Tell me something about yourself.
2. Is there anything else I should know about you?
3. How would you describe your character?
4. What do you want to do with your life?
5. How would you rate yourself on a scale of one to ten?
6. What year did you graduate?
7. Don't you think you're overqualified for this position?
8. What are your pet peeves?
9. Do you think you're unique?
10. What was the last book you read?
11. What was the last movie you saw?
12. Are you a happy person?
13. What types of things make you angry?
14. In what ways are you similar or different from your best friend?
15. How do you deal with rejection?
16. How do you deal with tension?
17. What would you do if money were not a concern?
18. Are you a natural leader or a natural follower?
19. How do you cope with change?
20. What personal attributes do you have for success in your field?
21. What kinds of people do you have problems working with?
22. What kinds of people do you like working with?
23. How have you shown willingness to work?
24. Do you interact well with people?
25. How do you get along with superiors?
26. Do you get along with co-workers?
27. Do you get along with people that you've supervised?
28. Do you generally think of yourself as a risk-taker or someone who plays it safe?

29. How would your co-workers describe you?
30. What do you do when you're having a problem with a co-worker?
31. What kind of people do you find it most difficult to get along with?
32. If you could change one thing about your personality, what would it be? Why?
33. What problems do you have tolerating people different from you?
34. How tolerant are you of others' opinions?
35. What are some areas you disagreed with your supervisor?
36. What do you like to do with your spare time?
37. What are some of your outside interests or hobbies?
38. What working relationship outside of the company have you handled successfully?
39. How would you describe your relationship with your last few supervisors?
40. How do you feel about your current employer?
41. What do your subordinates think of you?
42. What is your best personality trait?
43. What is your worst personality trait?
44. How would one of your friends describe you?
45. If you could improve two things about yourself, what would they be?
46. In what ways do you deal with criticism?
47. Do you classify yourself as a risk-taker?
48. In relation to others, how do you view yourself on taking initiative?
49. What are your motivations?
50. Do you see yourself as predictable?
51. Are you a better leader or follower?
52. Which person has had the most influence on your life?
53. Are you a trusting person, or do you reserve judgment?
54. Have you ever been openly criticized?
55. Have you ever openly criticized someone else?
56. How would you work with someone you didn't like?
57. Do you like working with numbers?
58. Do you like working with computers?
59. Do you like working with people?
60. Who has been an inspiration to you?

61. Do you consider yourself competitive?
62. Do you consider yourself intelligent?
63. Do you see yourself as more technically or management oriented?
64. What types of situations really depress you?
65. How would your best friend describe you?
66. Do you live to work or work to live?
67. What are your personal short and long-term goals?
68. What are your personal five-year goals?
69. Do you agree that others should use the same criteria as you in making choices?
70. How would you change your planning for your future if you could?
71. How well do you work under pressure?
72. How would you define drive?
73. How would you define motivation?
74. How would you define confidence?
75. How would you define integrity?
76. How would you define determination?
77. How would you define professionalism?
78. How are you improving yourself?
79. Have you ever put your own needs aside to help a co-worker?
80. Do your subordinates come to you with personal problems?
81. Would you be happy in an entry-level job?
82. What kind of boss do you prefer?
83. Do you trust your co-workers' advice?
84. How would you describe yourself?
85. What is the toughest part of a job?
86. What are your strong points?
87. How would you describe success?
88. Are you a successful person?

WORK AND MANAGEMENT SKILLS

89. What do you see as the role of a supervisor?
90. Can you work under pressure?
91. Are you a leader?
92. What are the benefits of training?
93. Are you a good manager?

INTERVIEW QUESTIONS 11-5

94. How hard do you work to achieve your objectives?
95. How would you resolve a conflict on a project team?
96. What do your employees think of you?
97. What is your biggest weakness as a manager?
98. What are your long-range career goals?
99. How do you measure productivity?
100. What would prevent you from becoming a good supervisor?
101. What qualities did you like in your previous supervisor?
102. How would you utilize your time as a supervisor?
103. Explain your philosophy on discipline?
104. Explain the methodology of problem solving?
105. How would you effectively motivate a problem employee?
106. What is the most important management issue today?
107. Have you overlooked any potential problems as a manager?
108. What are the most important aspects of a manager?
109. How would you handle a marginal performer?
110. How can you increase morale?
111. How would you handle low productivity?
112. What is the biggest problem with your company?
113. What is one of your greatest accomplishments?
114. How will you handle an employee who is constantly late for work?
115. How have you prepared yourself for the position you are applying?
116. How would you handle the employee who has a drug or alcohol problem?
117. What are the duties and responsibilities of the position you are applying?
118. What are the characteristics that you would want your subordinates to possess?
119. What do you believe is the most important characteristic or quality of a supervisor?
120. Explain your philosophy regarding effectiveness versus efficiency?
121. What are some of the indicators of the level of morale within an organization?
122. How would you increase morale in an organization?
123. What are your greatest strengths?
124. What are your greatest weaknesses?
125. How do you resolve conflicts?

126. What are your team-player attributes?
127. How do you handle leadership?
128. How would you set the goals and objectives for your employees?
129. How will you know if the goals and objectives were being achieved?
130. How will you measure the achievement of the goals and objectives you have set?
131. How do you deal with interpersonal conflict?
132. What's the toughest problem you've ever solved?
133. What challenges have you faced in a leadership position?
134. What was a team project that you helped complete?
135. What techniques do you use to motivate people?
136. How do you deal with pressure situations?
137. What pressure situations have you been involved with?
138. What difficult decisions have you made?
139. How do you persuade people to your point of view?
140. What is your biggest professional challenge?
141. How do you deal with failure?
142. What do you find frustrating?
143. How do you react when your honesty is questioned?
144. How do you plan to correct your weaknesses?
145. What skills do you most need to develop?
146. Are you willing to take risks?
147. Can you take instructions?
148. How effective are you under pressure?
149. How well do you cooperate?
150. What difficult problems have you dealt with?
151. Do you have attention to detail?
152. Do you prefer to work alone or with others?
153. What are your working methods?
154. Have you had problems getting along with others?
155. Have you successfully dealt with difficult people?
156. How do you deal with people at different levels?
157. How do you prepare for major projects?
158. How do you handle directions?
159. How do you handle change?
160. What skills do you think you need to improve?
161. What do you find tough to do?
162. What decisions are difficult for you?

163. What do you consider to be your greatest asset?
164. How do you feel your subordinates would describe you as a communicator?
165. How would you characterize your leadership and use of authority?
166. Were there any difficulties you overcame in achieving your accomplishments?
167. What have you learned on your current job?
168. What have you learned from your jobs?
169. How do you feel that you've improved your planning process in the last few years?
170. What important recommendations or decisions have you made recently?
171. What types of decisions are the most difficult for you to make?
172. How would you handle a decision for which no procedure existed?
173. What factors do you think have contributed to your effectiveness as a supervisor?
174. How do you handle criticism?
175. What are your most outstanding traits?
176. Are you a very organized person?
177. Do you manage your time well?
178. What do you do when faced with an important decision?
179. Describe how you work under pressure.
180. Do you anticipate problems effectively or just react to them?
181. Are you an innovator?
182. What are the skills you need to work on most?
183. How should disciplinary problems be dealt with?
184. How can disciplinary problems be avoided?
185. What interpersonal skills do you possess?
186. Do you have the ability to assume responsibility?
187. What about your performance in particular do your bosses tend to criticize most?
188. What were the results of your last performance appraisal?
189. What were the key strengths and weaknesses mentioned by your boss?
190. How do you handle conflicts?
191. Describe your management philosophy.

192. Have your disappointments helped you improve yourself?
193. Do you consider yourself creative?
194. Do you consider yourself analytical?
195. How organized are you?
196. How do you organize your time?
197. How would you compare your verbal and writing skills?
198. Do you work well in pressure situations?
199. How would you handle an angry customer?
200. How would you handle an angry supervisor?
201. What are some of the negatives stress can cause in the work environment?
202. How do you keep track of projects?
203. What factors would you use to predict a product's performance in the marketplace?
204. How would you complete an assignment that you resent doing?
205. How would you clarify an unclear assignment?
206. How do you go about making a decision?
207. How do you fix unexpected problems?
208. How would you deal with a subordinate who violated a company policy?
209. How would you help a co-worker with a personal problem?
210. How would you define your management philosophy?
211. What would you do if some team members weren't doing their share of the work?
212. How do you delegate responsibility?
213. How would you get subordinates who didn't like each other to work together?
214. What was your most creative idea?
215. Your supervisor tells you to do something in a way you know is ineffective. What would you do?
216. Your supervisor left you an assignment, then left town for a week. Now, you can't reach him and don't understand the assignment. What would you do?
217. How will you handle a subordinate who has made you aware that he or she is having martial difficulties?
218. When motivating a subordinate, what positive and negative factors would you include?
219. How would you have your subordinates participate in the decision making process and where do you draw the line

220. Have you handled fiscal duties?
221. You are a newly promoted supervisor and find most of your subordinates are simply ignoring your directives, what would you do?
222. Why do you want to become a supervisor, and why should you be chosen over the other candidates?
223. What do you see as the most effective style of management and the worst style of management?
224. Who is the most important in a disciplinary proceeding, the employee or the company?
225. An employee under your supervision has a negative attitude concerning the company, what would you do?
226. What would you propose be done in order to prevent sexual harassment from occurring in your workplace?
227. How would you handle a jealous employee that makes belittling comments under his breath that are directed toward you any time you attempt to conduct a meeting with the other employees?
228. You feel as though one of your employees may be experiencing some job-related stress. You are concerned about him because you know of the negative impact stress can have in the workplace. What signs, if any, would you look for in determining if someone is experiencing stress or a stress related syndrome?
229. What recommendations would you offer someone to help him or her alleviate the problems associated with stress?
230. Your department announces a new type of program to be initiated to combat an ongoing problem. Due to your experience, you know that this program has been tried in other departments and has failed miserably. What would you do and how will you present this program to your employees?
231. Part of your job as a supervisor is to monitor your employees for psychological changes that may affect their performance. What tools would you use to monitor these changes?
232. Discuss the rating criteria you would use in evaluating personnel under your supervision?
233. How do you organize your workload?

234. You have been assigned by the company's CEO to develop a program to enhance your department's hiring of minorities. What steps would you take in the development of the program?

BUSINESS AND POSITION PROFILE
235. What are your goals and your plans for reaching them?
236. Why are you interested in our company?
237. What do you know about our company?
238. What trends do you see occurring in our industry?
239. What is most important to you in a job?
240. What kind of job are you looking for?
241. What interests you about this company?
242. What concerns you about this company?
243. What are the most important attributes for this position?
244. What are you expecting from an employer?
245. What are the most important attributes of a good manager?
246. What challenges are you looking for in a job?
247. How can you contribute to this company?
248. Why would you like this line of work?
249. Why should I hire you?
250. What are the elements that make a good manager?
251. How would you define directing?
252. How would you define planning?
253. How would you define organizing?
254. How would you define coordinating?
255. How would you define discipline?
256. What will be the determining factors in choosing a job?
257. Why are you the best person for the position?
258. How does this job fit into the goals of the company?
259. Do you have a problem with routine tasks?
260. How long would it take you to start contributing to our company?
261. What would you define as a conducive work atmosphere?
262. What do you find least interesting about this job?
263. What do you find most interesting about this job?
264. What aspects of the job are the most important?
265. What can you do for us that no one else can?
266. What are you looking for in a job?

INTERVIEW QUESTIONS 11-11

267. What's the most important thing you're looking for in a job?
268. Why do you want to work here?
269. What are your future career plans?
270. What do you hope to be doing five years from now?
271. What do you know about this company?
272. Where do you see yourself in ten years?
273. What are some things you'd like to accomplish in life?
274. What are your future career goals and how do you hope to achieve them?
275. When would you expect a promotion?
276. Why are you interested in this position?
277. What do you like about our company the most?
278. What do you dislike about our company?
279. How do you see your work methods in comparison to ours?
280. What type of responsibilities in your job would you like to see added?
281. Which do you want more now, career growth or a change of pace?
282. What does "success" mean to you?
283. What does "failure" mean to you?
284. What do you feel makes you qualified for this job?
285. What would you change about your current job or position?
286. What do you feel would be an acceptable attendance record?
287. What are your qualifications?
288. What are you hidden professional attributes?
289. Are you a good listener?
290. What is your energy level?
291. What can you bring to this company?
292. How would you describe your standards of performance?
293. How do you handle the least exciting or least pleasant tasks that are part of this job?
294. Do you require close supervision?
295. How would you define your profession?
296. How would you determine progress in a good company?
297. What position are you interested in?
298. Do you consider yourself a professional?
299. Why do you feel that you're qualified for this job?

300. Would you rate yourself as an overachiever?
301. What is our company's mission statement?
302. What is your mission statement?
303. What direction do you think this company is headed in?
304. What do you know about our competitors?
305. How would we benefit if we hired you?
306. What are your opinions on the challenges facing our company?
307. What can you tell me about our company?
308. What can you tell me about our products?
309. What can you tell me about our company goals?
310. Why did you interview with this company?
311. Will you have the kind of time this position needs to be effective?
312. Where would you take your department if you got this position?
313. How would you organize your staff if you managed this operation?
314. What kind of job do you want immediately?
315. What characteristics do you look for in hiring?
316. What experience do you have for this job?
317. Why do you want to work for us?
318. If you could change something about this position, what would it be?
319. What do you see as your optimal career path?
320. If you were hiring, what type of person would you want to fill this position?
321. What changes do you see this industry making in order to stay competitive?
322. Could you give me three reasons why you're better than the other candidates?
323. How could you contribute to our company?
324. Why do you want this position?
325. What advantages do you think we have over our competitors?
326. What advantages do you think our competitors have over us?
327. What single aspect of our company interests you the most?
328. What special qualifications do you have for this position?

INTERVIEW QUESTIONS 11-13

329. What do you know about our operation?
330. What specific ways can our company benefit from hiring you?
331. How important to you is the prospect for advancement?
332. What do you think are the biggest challenges you'll face in this position?
333. What kind of position are you looking for?
334. What are the qualities that are most important to a manager?
335. Why do you feel that you can be successful in this position?
336. What part of your workload do you find most challenging?
337. How would you change your current working conditions?
338. What is your definition of stress?
339. What does it take to be professional?
340. What are the most important characteristics you are looking for in a job and why?
341. Do you feel qualified to be successful in your position?
342. What will you do to compensate for your deficiencies?
343. What are your professional five-year goals?
344. What are the most important things you want to get out of a job?
345. How do you think supervisors and subordinates should act toward one another?
346. What aspects of the job do you believe are the most important?
347. What characteristics do you think a person must have to be successful in your field?
348. If your job description were changed after we hired you, how would you respond?
349. The successful candidate for this position will be working with some highly trained individuals who have been here for a long time. How will you fit in?
350. Which of the following matters most in deciding to take the job: money, recognition, challenge, or responsibility?
351. What story could you tell me that would make you stand out from the other candidates?
352. What is the most intellectually stimulating thing you are looking for in a job and why?
353. What qualities make the best manager?

354. How do you see your position as a stepping stone to the further development of your career?
355. If I hired you for this position, what responsibilities do you most look forward to filling?
356. If you could construct your own job within our company, what factors would you include?
357. What are your greatest strengths and weaknesses and how will they affect your performance here?
358. What do you believe to be the prime factor that allows people to succeed in business today?
359. What do you hope to find in your next job that you can not find in your present position?

SALARY QUESTIONS
360. What salary were you thinking of earning for this position?
361. What do you think would make a fair compensation package for this position?
362. How much compensation will it take to get you here?
363. Why do you think you deserve your current salary?
364. Would you be willing to work for less?
365. How much money would you like to be earning?
366. How much money do you see yourself making in ten years?
367. Are you aware that this job might entail a cut in pay?
368. Why are you willing to take a cut in pay?
369. What salary do you expect?
370. Would you take a cut in salary to work here?
371. What are your current salary requirements?
372. How do you see your salary requirements changing in the near and far futures?
373. Do you feel that money is the most important aspect of a job?
374. How much do you expect to be earning in five years?
375. How much do you expect to be earning in ten years?

PROFESSIONAL EXPERIENCE PROFILE
376. What's been the greatest influence on your career plans?
377. What work experience has helped you the most?
378. What criticism of you has helped you the most?
379. Has your work experience prepared you for this position?

INTERVIEW QUESTIONS 11-15

380. What have been your biggest accomplishments?
381. Why did you leave your last job?
382. Why do you want to leave your present job?
383. Are you still employed?
384. Why do you want to leave your current employer so soon?
385. Do you think you've been with one company for too long?
386. What management positions have you held?
387. What has been the biggest criticism of you?
388. What was the best boss you've ever had?
389. What was the worst boss you've ever had?
390. What was the most important lesson you've ever learned?
391. Can you give me an example of one of your failures?
392. What brought you to enter this field?
393. How did you choose this field to study?
394. What do you like most about your specialty?
395. What is missing from your last job that you would like to see in this one?
396. How closely have your past supervisors managed you?
397. How well do you get along with your co-workers?
398. With which departments did you mostly interact with in your first position?
399. Do you have any experience working to meet deadlines?
400. Could you tell me the biggest change you've brought to your present company?
401. What experience do you think makes the best employee? Manager?
402. Which are the most important areas that you control?
403. What specifically have you been doing since you entered this field?
404. What's your idea of the ultimate job?
405. Have you had any supervisory experience?
406. What experience do you have?
407. How did your boss rate your job performance?
408. What types of job experiences in your last position have angered you?
409. How did you spend most of your time in your last job?
410. How do you feel about your career progress?
411. How did you move up within the company?
412. What experience do you have for this job?
413. Why do you want to change positions?

414. Did you have any problems in your previous jobs?
415. What would your references say about you?
416. What is your present position?
417. What are the responsibilities of your position?
418. Name three references that are available for consultation.
419. May I contact your current employer?
420. Have you ever been in the position to hire anyone? Why did you choose them?
421. Have you ever been in the position to fire anyone? Why did you fire that person?
422. If you could start your career over, what would you do differently?
423. What is the biggest mistake you ever made in selecting a job? Why?
424. What exactly do you do for a living?
425. Have you had any other interviews?
426. How did you prepare for this interview?
427. Tell me about the best boss you've ever had.
428. Tell me about the worst boss you've ever had.
429. What have been the most memorable accomplishments of your career?
430. You have very little experience. How do you intend to learn?
431. Describe how your department is organized.
432. Did you implement any new procedures in any of the positions you've held?
433. Do you have experience with some of the greatest challenges that this industry faces?
434. Besides your education, what other areas of preparation do you have for this position?
435. Looking back now, is there anything that you could have done to improve your relationship with that one bad boss?
436. What is the title of the person who you report to, and what were his or her responsibilities?

EDUCATIONAL QUESTIONS
437. Has your education prepared you for this position?
438. Do you have a college degree?
439. Do you have an advanced degree?
440. What special licenses or certifications do you hold?

441. What has been the greatest single influence in your life?
442. Do you have any plans to continue your education?
443. How has your education prepared you for this career?
444. What seminars have you taken in the last five years to stay on the top of your field?
445. What educational goals do you currently have?
446. Are you planning to go to graduate school?
447. What have you learned that can be used on the job?
448. When did you decide on your major?
449. What did you like most about college?
450. What did you like least about college?
451. What is your overall GPA?
452. Have you ever received a grade lower than expected? What did you do about it?
453. For advancement, would you consider a higher degree?
454. What trade journals do you read?
455. Are grade point averages an indication of how successful you will be in your job?
456. What would you do differently in college?
457. What are your plans for furthering your education?
458. Now that you've had some real-world experience, would you change anything about your education?
459. What correlation do you see between grades in school and success in the workplace?

MISCELLANEOUS QUESTIONS

460. What honors have you received?
461. What awards have you received?
462. Why were you let go?
463. Why have you been out of work for so long?
464. Have you ever been asked to resign?
465. Have you changed jobs frequently?
466. Have you ever been fired for reasons that seem unfair?
467. Would you be willing to take a drug test?
468. Do you want your boss' job?
469. How long do you plan to work for this company?
470. What would you say about a supervisor who was unfair?
471. What would you say about a supervisor who was tough to work with?
472. What would you say if I said your presentation was awful?

473. How long have you been looking for a new job?
474. How many offers have you received?
475. What were your biggest failures?
476. Have you ever been reprimanded?
477. Have you ever been denied a promotion?
478. How have you ever embarrassed yourself?
479. Have you ever intentionally deceived someone?
480. For what period of time do you envision yourself working for our company?
481. How did you get the time off to interview?
482. What mistakes might we make in hiring you?
483. Give me one reason I should hire you over a more qualified candidate?
484. Have you ever been fired?
485. Have you ever been asked to resign?
486. Have you ever turned down a promotion?
487. Have you ever turned down a salary increase?
488. Your experience isn't exactly what we need right now, is it?
489. Did your former employer have any policies that you consider unfair?
490. Have you ever missed a deadline? Why?
491. What judgmental errors have you made?
492. How could you have prevented your judgmental errors?
493. Doesn't this job represent a step down from the level of work you have been doing?
494. Why do you want to leave your present job?
495. What is the reason behind your desire for a career change?
496. How important is job security to you?
497. What would you do if you had a decision to make and no procedure existed?
498. Have you ever been discriminated against or treated unfairly?
499. What assurances do we have that you will stay with this company?
500. Are there any physical limitations that you have which would limit your performance in this position?

INTERVIEW QUESTIONS 11-19

Well, how did you do? Did you find that many of the questions were similar in content, and thus your answers were similar? If your answer to the question is "yes," great. That's what we were trying to explain. With practice you will virtually be able to deal with any question or problem, and your confidence level will increase.

The listed interview questions are common ones. You may be asked to answer any of these questions during the course of your interview. Preparing answers for these questions and others you can think of will assist you in your comprehension, answering, and problem solving abilities. Virtually everyone can use interviewing practice. Rehearse until you can easily answer the questions with clarity, spontaneity, and crispness. Your preparation and practice will shine through. Take some time to get to know yourself and consider how you will be perceived in the business world. Your file cabinet of knowledge will enable you to draw from an assortment of work and management styles, key issues, and problem solving techniques to answer the questions with authority.

Success –
"The secret of success is constancy to purpose."
Benjamin Disraeli (1805-1881) Writer

11-20 THE PROMOTIONAL EDGE

COMMENTS/NOTES

Interviewing Tips   12

We have provided you with dozens upon dozens of interviewing tips and techniques throughout this book. Review the checklists detailed in the previous chapters. The following is a quick study in the art of the oral interviewing process. Use the quick study tips and techniques outlined below as a refresher guide, and you will be well on your way to a successful oral interview.

- ✓ If possible find out who will be interviewing you.
- ✓ Talk with others who have taken recent interviews about the type of questions they were asked and about their experiences in the oral interview.
- ✓ Study the position specifications in the job announcement.
- ✓ Think through each qualification required.
- ✓ Organize yourself.
- ✓ Research management and company material.
- ✓ Drill yourself with possible questions and answers.
- ✓ Try on your clothes and have them ready several days prior to the interview date.
- ✓ Get a good night's sleep.
- ✓ Watch your general health and mental attitude.
- ✓ Dress neat, clean, and be well-groomed.
- ✓ Arrive early to the interview location.
- ✓ Reflect upon your preparation and confidence level.
- ✓ Think positive. Tell yourself repeatedly – *"I will do great,"* *"I will get hired or promoted."*
- ✓ Pump yourself up. Be enthusiastic!!!
- ✓ Don't rush the introduction.

- ✓ Repeat the interviewer's name, if possible.
- ✓ Be natural.
- ✓ At all times be courteous.
- ✓ Be Yourself.
- ✓ Remember a relaxed appearance is impressive.
- ✓ Be attentive.
- ✓ Never interrupt the interviewer.
- ✓ Pause to gather your thoughts before every response.
- ✓ Make sure you understand the question.
- ✓ Be clear.
- ✓ Be concise.
- ✓ Use your Power Words.
- ✓ Explain your position, then expound upon your response showing your depth of thinking.
- ✓ Don't assume the interviewer can read you. Interviewers want to hear your explanations.
- ✓ Don't repeat yourself during the same question.
- ✓ Respond to the questions directly, then build upon your response and support your position with examples, statistics, and other pertinent data.
- ✓ Use the unlimited amount of resources you have available. Usually an interviewer will not put constraints on you, but don't over do it.
- ✓ Don't belabor your point. Say what is on your mind and stop.
- ✓ Be personal in your approach to employees.
- ✓ Let an interviewer know when you are finished. Briefly, sum up your ideas in a sentence or two.
- ✓ Be sensitive to the needs of the company's customer base.
- ✓ Don't be afraid to smile.
- ✓ Maintain comfortable eye contact, but don't stare.
- ✓ If there are more than one interviewer direct your answers to each interviewer, not just the one who asked the question.
- ✓ Don't be overly technical or ponderous.
- ✓ Never say anything negative during an interview.

INTERVIEWING TIPS 12-3

- ✓ Don't be afraid to use body language to make a point. Lean forward in your chair to drive home your position. Use your facial expressions effectively.
- ✓ Watch what causes the interviewers to write. Almost all notes are good comments about your responses.
- ✓ Don't be intimidated by probing or follow-up questions. They are normally asked to work in your favor or to examine your depth of thinking.
- ✓ Don't get discouraged if you cannot read an interviewer's body language. Remain positive, enthusiastic, and continue with your style.
- ✓ End with a brief, but positive Closing.
- ✓ Thank the interviewers for their time.
- ✓ Acknowledge and shake hands, and don't be afraid to smile to show your relief as your are about to leave.
- ✓ Never ask an interviewer how you did.
- ✓ Leave the interviewer with a positive impression of you.

Results-
"Everyone is bound to bear patiently the results of his own example." Phaedrus (8 A.D.) - Philosopher

12-4 THE PROMOTIONAL EDGE

COMMENTS/NOTES

Mock Oral Interview 13

MOCK ORAL INTERVIEW RATING FORM

Candidate: _____

Assessor: _____

SCALE:
4.0 - 5.0 = Superior
3.0 - 3.9 = Very Good
2.0 - 2.9 = Average
1.0 - 1.9 = Adequate
0.0 - 0.9 = Below Average

COMMUNICATION SKILLS

Expresses ideas clearly, concisely, and effectively _____

Listens attentively _____

Uses proper grammar _____

Displays self-assurance, appears unflustered _____

Is well organized _____

Is persuasive and enthusiastic _____

Uses gestures effectively (eye contact, hands, etc.) _____

Avoids using distracting verbal mannerisms _____

TOTAL _____

INTERPERSONAL SKILLS

Works harmoniously with others _____

Promotes cooperation _____

Maintains professional relationships _____

Exhibits sensitivity to the needs of others _____

Demonstrates poise and composure _____

Praises subordinates for quality of work performed _____

Investigates disputes/complaints on subordinates _____

Counsels subordinates when necessary _____

TOTAL _____

MOTIVATIONAL SKILLS

Has taken steps to broaden formal education _____

Has variety of experience from assignments _____

Enthusiastic about job and desired position _____

Creative in ways to motivate subordinates _____

Creates a positive work atmosphere _____

Promotes employees to achieve higher education _____

Stimulates creativity in subordinates _____

Assist subordinates in learning new skills _____

TOTAL _____

ABILITY TO ASSUME RESPONSIBLITY

Quickly defines the problem _____

Makes sound decisions promptly _____

Defends and stands behind decisions _____

Desire to get the job done at present level _____

Objectivity in stressful situations _____

Uses available resources to complete tasks _____

Innovative in problem solving _____

Solicits ideas from others for decision _____

TOTAL _____

LEADERSHIP SKILLS

Properly delegates tasks and assignments _____

Maintains necessary documentation _____

Plans future actions _____

Understands rules and regulations _____

Properly administers discipline _____

Keeps chain of command informed _____

Conducts appropriate follow-up _____

Understands the Big Picture _____

TOTAL _____

OVERALL SCORE: _____
(add total scores of all and divide by 2)

13-4 THE PROMOTIONAL EDGE

COMMENTS/NOTES

Conclusion 14

To paraphrase the late baseball great Yogi Berra, "When it's over it's over." You have done the best you can do. After the interview, relax. The rest is out of your hands. Feel good about yourself. Critique yourself, but never second-guess yourself. You will only drive yourself crazy thinking about all of the things you should have said. Learn from your experiences. You have put forth a tremendous amount of tiresome time and energy preparing, and eventually your commitment to yourself will pay off.

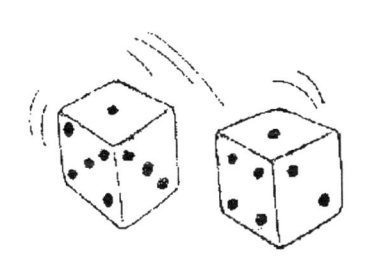

EVALUATING THE INTERVIEW

Every interview should be a learning experience. In order to improve upon your interview behavior and techniques, review what happened during your conversation with the interviewer. Ask yourself:

- How did the interview go?
- Did I miss any opportunities to sell myself?
- Did I present myself well?
- Did I find out what the company needed?
- Did I present my qualifications well?
- Was I too nervous?
- Did I appear confident?
- Did I talk too much or too little?
- Did I have difficulty answering certain questions?
- How can I improve myself for the next interview?

FOLLOW-UP

A brief thank you note has become customary after an interview. It is strongly recommended that you send a letter or note no later than the day following the interview. Do not, however, make repeated phone calls inquiring as to the status of the interview process. This may prove irritating to the interviewer and decrease your chances of getting the position.

CRITIQUE

Perform a self-critique of your interview performance immediately after the oral interview process. Record your thoughts about your own reactions, responses, and rapport. This will help you mentally close out the interview. Write down your strong selling points and those that need refining. List all questions that were asked so that you can develop improved answers for your next interview. With each interview, you will gradually develop greater self-confidence, project a more polished image, provide improved responses, refine your oral communication skills, and perfect your presentation techniques.

Use this book as a reference tool, but don't stop here. Build upon your resources to accomplish your goal. Securing the job of your dreams or a promotion is within your power and ability. The oral interview process isn't the crap-shoot everyone makes it out to be. Interviewing is merely a skill that can be practiced, perfected, and used to a tremendous advantage, time and time again. Job hunting or preparing for a promotion can be one of the most difficult tasks to overcome, but you must never give up. You now know the most effective interviewing techniques, but it is up to you to use them.

Remember, your mental state and attitude is half the battle. Enthusiasm begins with a positive mental attitude. If your attitude is negative there is no way you will be enthusiastic. You must exude confidence in who you are and what you do. Believe in yourself and you will succeed. Practice and perfect the necessary skills whenever possible, and very soon the most difficult job you will be facing is deciding how to celebrate your new found success. Oh, by the way, we are always open to invitations as long as the beer is cold.

Success -
"Some people want it to happen, some wish it to happen, others make it happen." Michael Jordan - N.B.A. Chicago Bulls

14-4 THE PROMOTIONAL EDGE

COMMENTS/NOTES

Final Note   15

We sincerely hope this book was of great assistance in helping you prepare for your oral interview. If you have any questions, comments, or suggestions about this book, whether good, bad, or indifferent, we would love to hear from you. We are forever attempting to update the material in order to help all of you succeed. Please drop us a line or send us an e-mail message to the address listed below. Remember, all victories have their foundation rooted in careful preparation. Good luck in your endeavors. We wish you much continued success.

Ron Bateman and Chuck Mounts

Promotional Edge Publishing
626C #220 Admiral Drive
Annapolis, Maryland 21401

E-Mail Address: **ProEdgePub@aol.com**

Index

Ability, 7-4
Accessories - dress, 9-5
Achievement oriented, 8-6
Achievements, 7-4
Anxiety, 2-2
Appearance, 9-10
Assertiveness, 8-7
Assessed areas, 7-3
  achievement, 7-7
  business profile, 7-5
  personal profile, 7-4
  professional profile, 7-5
Assessment, 7-1

Behavior, 9-8
Behavior-based
  interviews, 8-2
Belief in yourself, 2-4
Big day, 10-1
Blouses, 9-6
Bonding process, 10-3
Budgeting, 7-4
Business dress,
  men, 9-3
  women, 9-5
Business profile, 7-4

Career background,
  3-6, 3-7, 3-12
Chain of command,
  3-21, 5-4

Checklist, 9-9
  assessed areas, 7-4
  body language, 6-4
  dress, 9-9
  interviewing tips, 12-1
  stress, 2-4
Closing hints, 3-6
Closing statements,
  3-5, 3-24
Communication, 7-4
  effective, 4-1
  nonverbal messages,
    6-1
  skills, 3-5, 8-6
Conceptual knowledge, 1-8
Conclusion, 3-14, 14-1
Confide, 2-4
Confidence, 7-4, 7-10, 8-10
  revitalizing, 1-4
Conscientious, 8-7
Control, 7-8
Coordinating, 7-5
Critique, 5-1, 14-2

Dedication, 7-4, 7-5
Dependability, 8-7
Depression, 2-2
Determination, 7-4
Directing, 7-4
Direct interview, 8-2
Discipline, 3-22, 7-4

Documentation, 3-20, 5-3
Dress for men, 9-3
   accessories, 9-5
   shirt, 9-4
   shoes, 9-5
   socks, 9-4
   ties, 9-4
Dress for women, 9-5
   accessories, 9-6
   blouses, 9-6
Dressing sharp, 9-1
Drive, 7-4

EEOC, 8-5
Education, 7-4
Educational background, 3-6, 3-8, 3-12
Efficiency, 7-4
Emotionally stable, 8-7
Empathy, 8-7
Energetic, 7-4
Enthusiasm, 7-4, 10-10
Evaluating interviews, 14-1
Exercise, 2-4
Eye contact, 6-2, 10-2

Final note, 15-1
First impressions, 9-1
Follow-up, 3-23, 5-3, 14-2
Follow-up questions, 7-2

General interview, 8-2

Handshake, 10-2
Hired.- top ten, 7-9
Honors, 7-4

Imagination, 8-7
Inappropriate questions, 8-3
Integrity, 7-4
Intellectually curious, 8-7
Interpersonal skills, 7-4
Interviewers, 3-3
Interviews, 7-2
   direct, 8-2
   non-direct, 8-2
   behavior-based, 8-2
Interview questions, 11-1
Interviewing tips, 12-1
Introduction, 1-1

Job announcement, 8-7
Job skills, 7-3

Key points, 8-7
Knowledge, 6-5
   conceptual, 1-8
   technical, 1-8
Knowledge Base, 1-8

Leadership skills, 13-3
Learning, 4-6
Listening skills, 7-4

Management skills, 7-4
Manner, 9-8
Mental relaxation, 2-5
Mirroring, 6-4
Miscellaneous tips, 9-7
Mock oral interview, 13-1
Motivation, 7-4

Non-direct interview, 8-2

INDEX 16-3

Nonverbal messages, 6-1
  eyes, 6-2
  facial expressions, 6-2
  head, 6-3
  miscellaneous, 6-3
  mouth, 6-3
  negative, 6-4
  positive, 6-4

Opening hints, 3-6
Opening statement,
  3-5, 3-12
Optimistic, 8-7
Oral interview day, 10-1
Oral interview parameters,
  7-1
Organizing, 7-4
Outlining your resume, 3-8

Parameters, 7-1
Personal profile, 7-4
Planning, 7-4
Points of interest,
  3-6, 3-9, 3-14
Position, 3-2
Positive resilience, 8-7
Power phrases, 4-5
Power words, 4-1
Praise, 3-22, 5-3
Preparation, 3-1, 3-25, 3-31
  benefits to, 1-6
  for the unknown, 1-5
Pride, 7-4
Problem solving techniques,
  3-16
  practice, 3-30

Professional skills, 7-4

Qualities, 8-1
Questions, 11-1
  business profile, 11-10
  critique, 5-1
  educational, 11-16
  follow-up, 7-2
  formulating, 3-26
  inappropriate, 8-3
  interview, 3-15, 11-1
  miscellaneous, 11-17
  professional profile,
    11-14
  salary, 11-14
  work & management
    skills, 11-5
Question techniques, 8-2

Reasons for failing an
  interview, 1-6
Reasons for getting hired,
  7-9
Research, 3-3
Responses, 7-7
Responsibility, 8-7
Results, 12-3
Resume, 3-8
Role as a manager, 3-4
Rules of the game, 8-9

Scheduling, 3-1
Self-confidence, 2-6
Self-control, 8-7
Shirts, 9-4
Shoes, 9-5

Sizing up the situation, 7-10
Skills, 3-4
Sociable, 8-7
Socks, 9-4
Staffing, 7-4
Steps, 3-1
    problem solving, 3-16
Stress, 2-1
    anticipatory stress, 2-3
    interview, 8-3
    points to remember, 2-4
    situational stress, 2-3
    time stress, 2-3
    warning signs, 2-2
Success factors, 7-9

Success, 5-9, 14-3

Taking control, 7-9
Technical Knowledge, 1-8
Tension, 2-2
Think positive, 2-4
Ties, 9-4
Tolerance, 8-7
Training, 7-4
Trustworthiness, 8-7
Types of interviews, 8-1

Work experience, 7-5

Your Delivery, 3-10

THE PROMOTIONAL EDGE
The Complete Guide to the Successful Oral Interview

Please complete the following to order additional copies. Quantity discounts are available.

Name _____

Address _____

City, State, Zip _____

Phone _____

THE PROMOTIONAL EDGE
The Complete Guide to the Successful Oral Interview

Number of copies _____ @ $12.95 each $ _____

Postage and handling @ $3.00 per order $ _____

Total amount enclosed $ _____

Please send and make checks payable to:

Promotional Edge Publishing
626-C #220 Admiral Drive
Annapolis, Maryland 21401